DANCING HEART TO HEART

The Story of RoHun^{SM}

By
ZOLAR

With Introduction By
Christian Tal Schaller, M.D.

We have chosen to use colored ink to reach both sides of the brain hemispheres so that your intution will be functioning in harmony with your intellect.

Look into any man's heart you please, and you will always find, in every one, at least one black spot which he has to keep concealed.

...HENRIK IBSEN, Pillars of Society

Editions Soleil - USA

The "Editions Soleil - USA" is the American branch of EDITIONS VIVEZ SOLEIL, a Swiss publishing company that is a pioneer in the field of health education. Its purpose is to promote the idea that "health can be learned" and to give tools to those who want to improve the quality of their physical, emotional, mental and spiritual life. With elegance, simplicity and humor the Soleil material presents the complementary of all schools of thought, from traditional medicines to scientific and spiritual knowledge.

A team of medical doctors, scientists, educators, artists and writers has been researching extensively since 1974 to present high quality information about how to achieve total health. The Soleil material give access to universal wisdom. It does not get outdated but will stay with their readers as life's companions. Soleil shows how to listen to the inner divine child, to live free of suffering and diseases, to experience vibrant vitality and health, to have more and more fun and joy, to open the intuition and creativity and to allow the inner artist to blossom.

Soleil will help you to enjoy your uniqueness and express your beauty through thoughts, words, deeds and art. Join the hundreds of thousands of people who are already creating a positive life for themselves and their family. Let the sun of well-being and happiness rise in the sky of your daily life!

Editions Soleil - USA works in synergy with DELPHI, an educational centre in McCaysville, Georgia and with many other centres around the world.

CONTENTS

FOREWORD
By
Christian Tal Schaller, M.D.

I became interested in RoHun after having spent many years as a general practitioner involved with psycho-therapy.

At the time I was working with a technique called "Day Dreaming," which in fact is very close to RoHun.

The purpose was to bring dynamics into the image of the patient by going into the psyche to see what they were using, and then to make it work by them finding the solution, instead of their following that imposed by the therapist.

What I liked about the process is that the therapist did not care what the image meant, but rather, simply that it was blocked and then helped the patient unlock it his own way. Certainly, what works for one may not work for another!

In twenty years I have been through various methods and techniques, but have never found something so simple as the RoHun process, which always gives power to the patient and not to the therapist.

The key to every therapy is "Who" do you empower!

What I like most is that when the RoHun therapist starts; he becomes totally empty. He does not start from a preconceived idea of what is good or bad, but rather lets himself be guided by the patient. In a manner of speaking, this method gives the hungry patient a fishing pole rather than just a fish to eat!

As therapists, we never know exactly what the solution is for someone. The only way people can really heal is by a self-process.

Most therapies attempt to place people into what they hold as normal, or right, or wrong. For example, if one says the average or normal size foot is nine, then everyone must wear the same size shoe, which cannot possibly work!

What I like about RoHun is that it provides a tool with which the patient does the work, while the therapist simply supports the process, without imposing his or her personal views. I find this very powerful!

These days one also hears a great deal about the process called <u>channeling</u>. While RoHun incorporates this process as part of its technique, the therapist does not channel information received from outside the patient. Rather, through the RoHun process, the patient develops his own ability to tune into that which has meaning for him and his life.

Unlike other therapies, RoHun is totally spontaneous with neither the patient nor the therapist knowing in advance what may arise. Hence, you are living totally in the now.

RoHun is an adventure with the therapist getting as much out of each session as the patient. There is a tremendous power which emerges when the therapist becomes so humble. No longer is he or she the one to say, "I know. I am going to fix it!" Rather, the attitude is, "I am one with you."

The function of the RoHun therapist is to let the patient make the discovery and to support that, instead of forcing him to accept his way which, unfortunately, is what many therapies do in order to maintain their rigid system.

Because of the unique structure of the RoHun process, there are often moments in which there is a resonance between the patient and the therapist. While a therapist usually attracts people with those problems he himself needs to solve, the beauty of this process is that when the patient gets something done, it hits the therapist as well, as he or she is always in the patient's energy field.

In other traditional therapies, the therapist's problems block the understanding and growth of the patient, which is decidedly not so with RoHun.

This is why it is often said in RoHun, "We are many, we are one." It is no longer one therapy and one patient. With RoHun, it is two beings who are getting in touch with the same energy, so that it does not matter who does what!

This is especially so since the connection between the two is through the heart. What you feel, I feel. What I feel, you feel.

As the RoHun process is intuitional, rather than intellectual or academic, the therapist continually purifies and enhances himself, as well as the patient, each time a session takes place. Spiritual energies are powerful ... and this is what you work with!

Also, as the RoHun therapist always begins each session by asking to be used as a channel of light, so that the patient may heal himself; he cannot play his own ego game at the same time. To try to do so would only enmesh him deeper, in his own stuff, to the detriment of the patient.

So it is that RoHun is unique in that it allows one to gain access to the experience of channeling through a method which does not allow one to indulge in his own ego trip. For this reason, some would-be RoHun therapists have abandoned the use of the technique, since they could no longer have power over their patients.

It is almost as if there is a built-in "initiation" process in the RoHun technique that only allows it to be used well, or not at all!

While anyone can benefit from the RoHun training, the main beneficiaries are those persons who are already therapists. Its technique brings a new dimension to the therapy they are doing, by adding the experiential connection to Spirit.

Instead of being exhausted at the end of the day, which is normal for most therapists, the RoHun practitioner finds himself the recipient of continuous spiritual energy throughout every session. Thus, RoHun reverses the usual pattern of the therapist being trapped and drained by his or her patients.

The only way to do good therapy is to learn to tap into a Higher Source of power, so you don't take your own energy. If I have a lamp, I prefer to plug it into the wall socket, rather than to pedal a bicycle to make my own current!

RoHun is really not for beginners.

Rather, it comes at the right moment when someone is ready to enter the spiritual path.

As a unique therapy, it provides a way to do it and to work with psychological blocks in a way which is never heavy, and that is outside any power games.

In the finality, the major feature of its process is the use of the heart. When people use the heart, everything falls into place. When you don't work with the heart, and work with the mind instead, one's problems only increase.

For me the whole beauty of the RoHun system is that it has been developed by people who have a tremendous amount of experience in the psychic field. But then they went into the heart connection ... which is quite another story!

To my way of thinking, the essence of spirituality is really to do things with pleasure and joy, and to have fun. We can only get this when we go through the heart.

For this reason, RoHun is clearly the psychotherapy of the future, because it saves a tremendous amount of time by going directly to that thought pattern which is the source of each and every problem.

One does not waste time interpreting, or thinking he must spend years reliving his old patterns.

Rather, one simply reaches the wrong thought and corrects it!

Tal Schaller, M.D.
DELPHI RETREAT CENTER
December 1989

A CHAT WITH ZOLAR

It seems almost like yesterday. The year was 1986. I was living in New York City at the time and busy at work on "BOOK OF THE SPIRITS." By coincidence, a neighbor of mine, Laurel Tower, had recently visited Key West. While there she had made friends with Renate Perelom who, unbeknownst to me, was a RoHun practitioner. Laurel told me of her first meeting with Renate and suggested that I meet her, too.

Now she was coming to town, and would be here a few days before going off to study at a place called Lily Dale, near Buffalo, New York!

Strange words these were to me ... RoHun ... Lily Dale! As events unfolded, it was because of Renate's visit and our meeting that I decided to travel to Lily Dale to interview many of the mediums who were living there.

It was at Lily Dale that I first met Patricia Hayes and her husband, Marshall Smith. The result of our meeting, of course, was the appearance of a chapter on Patricia and her work which later appeared in that book. If you, the reader, are not familiar with that book, which is a detailed history of spiritualism, mediumship and channeling, I suggest you run out right now and purchase a copy. It's easy to find. I have trained my children to place it at the very top of the shelf, at eye level, whenever they visit a bookstore!

Seriously, if you don't have a copy of this work, you should. It will greatly help your understanding of what is to follow in this particular work. For, you see, when I met Patricia and Marshall, I also met Dr. RoHun. Only I never dreamed, because of that chance meeting, I would now be writing an entire work on him and his work through Patricia.

So much has happened in just three short years. No longer is RoHun the private pearl of great price, possessed only by an inner circle of graduates of the Arthur Ford Academy, which Patricia founded many years ago. Instead, RoHun has found endorsement by therapists worldwide, including, of all people...psychiatrists and psychologists. Surely, if those who have access to any kind of therapy they wish are becoming students of RoHun, and using the technique in their own practice, there must be something to it.

As Granny would say, the proof of the pudding must be in the eating! Needless to say, I was both honored and intrigued when asked by Patricia and her associates to pen a complete work on this timely, unique therapy.

As always, it is my personal wish that ZOLAR's ever faithful readers will find presented in these few pages all they may need to know to decide if RoHun can change their lives as it has the lives of so many already.

Certainly, not everyone reading this work is a practicing psychotherapist, psychiatrist or psychologist. In fact, I would expect that many now reading these words are simply doing so out of some kind of curiosity. Perhaps the title of the work has caught their attention. For instance, what could he possibly mean by, "Dancing Heart To Heart?"

When I was a beginning student of metaphysics (too many years ago to remember), I was told that from ancient times the belief existed that, "When the disciple is ready, the Master will appear." In my naivete, I thought this meant that I would soon meet an old, gray haired man who would give me all the answers to the universe, personally, quickly ... and at a low cost! It was only through the passage of time that I came to realize that the word "Master" did not necessarily mean a person, but rather a state of mind, out of which wisdom could come. In other words ... an idea!

So, it may very well be that someone, somewhere, right now is reading this book. And that as a result, their life will be changed. You see, this is really what RoHun is all about. This is why this book had to be written.

Almost two thousand years ago, the Great Master wrote:

> *Neither do men light a candle, and put it under a bushel, but on a candlestick; and it giveth light unto all that are in the house.*

(Matt. 5:15)

In other words, truly the time has come to share a most remarkable process, whereby all the hurts of this life and 'others' can be healed in an extraordinarily short time.

Exactly how such a miracle can take place, dear reader, you will find in the pages that follow. I only hope that you will not stop with the reading of this book, but if you are so inclined, you will actively seek out the services of a RoHun practitioner...or certainly begin those studies so you may become one yourself!

Yes, the proof of the pudding is always in the eating. But this assumes that one will always eat!

The freedom to be healed is always yours...

There have never been incurable illnesses ... only incurable people!

ZOLAR
Key West, Florida
Winter, 1990

CHAPTER ONE

"DR. ROHUN ... I PRESUME?"

Thus we see that our conquest of disease will mainly depend on the following: firstly, the realization of the Divinity within our nature and our consequent power to over-come all that is wrong: secondly, the knowledge that the basic cause of disease is due to disharmony between the person-ality and the Soul; thirdly, our willingness and ability to discover the fault which is causing such a conflict; and fourthly, the removal of any such fault by developing the opposing virtue.

Dr. Edward Bach, HEAL THYSELF

Reference has already been made to my very first meeting with Dr. RoHun through Patricia Hayes in my work, "BOOK OF THE SPIRITS" (*Prentice Hall Press*).

Without a retelling of this story, it will suffice to say to those interested in such things that they should certainly make themselves familiar with this classic work.

As for Patricia's first meeting with Dr. RoHun, her work, "THE GATEKEEPER," published in 1981, best tells the story.

While I do not wish to waste space in the current work retelling this unusual tale, a few words must nonetheless be said about this meeting so you, the reader, may compre-hend what is to follow!

To begin with, it must be stated that Dr. RoHun only came to Patricia after a long period of prayer and medita-tion, during which time she first made contact with a spiritual entity who called himself simply, the Gatekeeper.

Much to her surprise, it was he who introduced her to Dr. RoHun, from whom she would begin to learn the various techniques which would eventually comprise the powerful and unique philosophy of healing that now bears his name.

To those reading this work, who do not accept the idea that such a spiritual contact can be made by anyone who masters certain, specific techniques, I can only say, "Be patient and read on." Hopefully, by the end of this work you, too, will believe as I now do.

At the onset of their first meeting, Dr. RoHun identified himself as a special kind of healer who headed a colony hospital on what he called the "fourth level."

His unusual task, he said, was to rehabilitate those souls who wish to continue their evolution, but who were blocked from this desire because they believed they would die a second death, as their illness was terminal.

The error, according to Dr. RoHun, was simply that they were still living with the third dimensional awareness that they were ill to begin with.

They had failed to realize that as they "thought," so were they!

Dr. RoHun went on to tell Patricia that his staff coun-seled these patients, who attended class each day, and that the key to their total healing lied in simply removing the memory of their illness!

While ideas such as these are certainly nothing new to the world of metaphysics, Dr. RoHun then went on to present Patricia with the very first of many techniques for actually removing illness.

More than just profound were these words concerning the real nature of disease:

Some use disease for their own purposes. Disease is a way of being a martyr. Disease is a way for people to express the idea that others should feel sorry for them. Disease is also a way of punishing self. Disease can be an escape. Disease is a habitual chronic habit for some that gives them a reason to be recognized. These are only a few of the reasons for disease.

When questioned by Patricia as to the origin of his name, Dr. RoHun simply replied, "We choose our names quite differently than you do. We choose the first sound of our name for the frequency of vibration and the second sound for our chosen mission."

The good doctor continued, "Ro will be recognized by others on the same frequency and Hun is my profession, which is the study of health."

While the idea of spirit doctors working with mediums is certainly not a new one, Patricia's contact with Dr. RoHun was soon to take a most unusual twist.

It was his wish that Patricia research here, on the third dimension, the conclusions that he and his staff, on the fourth dimension, had reached.

This he did by first presenting her with a technique for removing memories of an illness, which he claimed were stored within the chakras, an essential part of the subtle anatomy of man!

Later on we will discuss in depth the concept of the chakras, which plays an essential part to the philosophy of RoHun.

Needless to say, at first, Patricia found the energy of Dr. RoHun far beyond anything she had yet experienced.

Little did she know how his appearance would change her life, by providing her and her family with a mission of extraordinary importance.

Much to her amazement, and the delight of her eager students, each of the many techniques presented by Dr. RoHun actually worked to bring about miracles and psychological breakthroughs that often seemed uncanny!

It was almost as if Dr. RoHun was psychically present, almost as a Jungian archetype, at each RoHun session, ever guiding the therapist.

What began to unfold, after many months and years, was a totally integrated psychotherapy process, without equal in its speed and effectiveness to produce major breakthroughs for patients who had long struggled.

By artfully using the electromagnetic fields surrounding every person, therapist and client join in creative interaction to bring about an acceleration of consciousness. This interaction also clears out negative thought patterns which have long held the client in mental and spiritual bondage.

While the idea that "thoughts are things" is definitely an old metaphysical hat, what RoHun uniquely provides is an actual energy based technique that enables both the therapist and client to co-create new, positive patterns through a kind of "thought surgery."

Thoughts that have attracted pain, hurt, chaos, isolation are cleansed and removed, one by one, from the various chakras in which they laid hidden for many lifetimes.

Yes ... one of the many discoveries that have come out of the RoHun experience ... is the fact that we have indeed lived many, many lives.

In fact, it may very well be an experience from "another time" or "another place" that now shackles us and keeps us from the joy and happiness we rightfully deserve as joint heirs to the Kingdom!

Later on, we will explore this idea in greater depth. As RoHun is a spiritually-based energy system of soul integration, it seeks to move each therapist and client from the recognition of the soul to the realization of Self.

Hence, those who experience and practice the techniques regularly ever increase their awareness from the finite to the infinite!

As the correction of faulty thought patterns is fundamental to the RoHun process, one might rightly ask, "What is a faulty thought?"

The simplicity of the answer may surprise you!

A faulty thought is any thought that prevents one from attaining greater experience, greater fulfillment and still greater success.

When a number of faulty thoughts are collected and bound together by the apparent repetition of similar experiences, they in a sense create a "faulty thought body," which continues to work through the unconscious mind to limit one's success in life.

Again, while there is nothing new to this particular idea, RoHun is unique in ascribing this blockage to the electromagnetic fields surrounding the physical, emotional and spiritual bodies of each person.

In other words, the key to releasing these faulty thought patterns lies in an understanding of the interrelationship between each individual and his or her own energy fields. It is the task of the therapist, then, to assist the client in clearing those thought patterns that attract negative life experiences.

Perhaps, an example will make this even more clear.

If one wrongly possesses the idea that, "I am not worthy," it follows that one may also believe:

> I am not capable of love.
> I feel alone.
> Nobody loves me.
> I can't trust anyone.
> I don't trust myself.
> I'm always rejected.

Let's try another example so you begin to get my gist. This time, let's start with the idea, "I am helpless." If this is true, then it must also be true that:

> I'm a victim.
> I resent those who make me feel helpless.
> I'm not intelligent enough.
> I need someone to do it for me.
> I can't do anything right.
> I can't do it myself.

Are you starting to see what I mean by a "faulty thought body?"

For good measure, let's try one more!

Let's now take what is no doubt the most commonly found faulty thought pattern of all ... "I am afraid!"

From this it is easy to see that it must follow that:

> I could lose what I have.
> If I love, I'll be rejected.
> I can't handle it.
> I'm afraid to express what I really feel.

> I have to keep people away, so
> people don't see me.
> If I try, I may fail.
> If I try, I may feel.

Now you may begin to see why we called one of the many processes RoHun works with, "Thought Surgery."

In a manner of speaking, much in the same way a skilled surgeon might remove a tumor that is preventing one's life force from its natural flow, so does the combined energy of the RoHun therapist and client seek out and remove similar blockages.

While this is certainly the goal of any psychotherapy, the difference between RoHun and more traditional approaches is that its process isolates precisely "where" such blockages are located in the subtle anatomy, and removes them as easily as one would pop balloons!

It is for this reason, and this reason alone, that the recommended typical three two-hour sessions, with one or more follow-up sessions, often yield results that take other therapies years to accomplish.

One might liken this rapid-acting psychotherapy to shooting flies with a laser guided rifle, instead of a shotgun full of buckshot!

But these are not the only benefits of this extraordinary process, which goes still further to:

> Awaken the client's sensitivity to his or
> her own inner resources.

> Introduce the client to his or her own
> creative intuitive abilities.

> Assist the client in relaxing tension.

Provide the client with deep and mean-
ingful insight into his or her own
spirituality.

Aid the client in developing and reinforc-
ing self-confidence.

Help the client to 'forgive' and 'release'
the past, thereby obtaining freedom
from guilt and resentment.

Direct the client toward a more open
expression of self.

Increase peace and harmony within the
client.

Increase the client's understanding and
compassion for self and others.

Help the client become more comfortable with self and feel stronger about
his or her ability to cope with life.

Open up the heart of the client, so he or
she can truly give and receive love.

So there you have it in a nutshell!

But pay particular notice to the very last of these
promises, namely, the "Opening of The Heart." For it is here
that we find the reason that RoHun is more than just an idea
whose time has come.

In the next chapter, we will examine why the "Way of
The Heart" is, ultimately, the only way in which true self-
realization and healing can take place.

I invite you to turn the page...quickly now!

CHAPTER TWO

DANCING HEART TO HEART

I have come unto thee, O Un-nefer, and I have brought the Osiris Ani unto thee. His heart hath been found righteous and it hath come forth from the balance; it hath not sinned against any god or goddess. Thoth hath weighed it according to the degree uttered unto him by the company of the gods; and it is very true and right. Grant unto him cakes and ale; and let him enter into thy presence; and may he be like unto the followers of Horus forever.
EGYPTIAN BOOK OF THE DEAD

While we have yet to discuss the chakras, or various psychic centers, which are essential to the philosophy of RoHun we must nonetheless now turn our attention to an understanding of the "heart" and its very important place in these teachings.

Later on, we will discuss the "heart center," when we focus on the chakras themselves. Recently, an extraordinary study on the kind of persons that fall victims to heart attacks made front page in the popular press. Dr. Redford Williams, a professor of psychiatry at Duke University Medical Center in Durham, North Carolina, released findings which identified for the first time what it was in the legendary "Type A" behavior that produced fatal heart attacks. Surprisingly, it was not the long ago identified impatience, ambition or work drive that everyone had traditionally blamed, but rather something else, often touted by metaphysicians ... ANGER!

In Williams' own words, "It's the anger: it sends your blood pressure skyrocketing. It provokes your body to create unhealthy chemicals. For hostile people, anger is a poison."

One should not just let anger out, according to Williams. Sure this will keep one from becoming depressed or possibly developing ulcers, but one must go still further.

One must avoid feeling angry in the first place. For if this is done, there is nothing to suppress! While this is somewhat sage advice, and is presented in great detail in his book, The Trusting Heart, what Dr. Williams does not say is how one can do it, when he cannot break the anger pattern.

This is where the RoHun process of releasing faulty thoughts from where they are imprisoned, comes in. Although it is good to finally see that modern medical science is beginning to accept the idea that thoughts truly hurt or truly heal, the idea that the heart is more than just a physical pump is found in antiquity.

Before so-called science, the heart was symbolized as both the essence and center of being. "Taking heart" meant to "be courageous" as moral courage was long held to reside in the heart!

In mystical symbolism, the heart combines with the rose and the lotus flower to symbolize the secret hiding place behind all material things. For instance, in alchemy, the heart was held to be the sun's image within man. In the ancient art of Numerology, one's heart numbers (derived from the vowels in one's name) are said to indicate the real identity of their possessor as opposed to the persona or mask which we all wear outwardly.

For the Ancient Egyptians, extreme care was taken to preserve the heart of the dead, so it could accompany the body of the deceased into the afterlife.

Of especial interest to students of RoHun is the fact that the Ancient Egyptians held that the hearts of the dead were actually weighed on a balance in the presence of Osiris.

The earliest known evidence of a belief that the dead would be judged for their conduct in life, in this most unusual manner, occurs in Egyptian texts dated about 2400 B.C.!

It was not until the Middle Kingdom (c2160-1580 B.C.), however, that we find in the so-called Coffin Texts the idea of an actual weighing on balances as the method of assessment. How this weighing was to be done was not clarified until the New Kingdom (c1580-1090 B.C.), however, at which time perhaps one of the most impressive representations, beautifully drawn and colored, was created.

Entitled the Papyrus of Ani, now the possession of the British Museum, the illustration depicts the dead scribe, Ani and his wife, watching the weighing of Ani's heart in what is called the Hall of Two Truths.

Central to the illustration is a great balance. On one scale-pan is the hieroglyphic symbol of the heart. On the other is an ostrich feather, symbolic of Maat or "truth."

In other words, Ani's heart, held by the ancient Egyptians to be an independent witness or censor, and not his acts or beliefs, must balance with "Truth" if he is to gain passage into the other world and eternal life!

Attending the fateful balance scene is Anubis, the jackal-headed mortuary god, who adjusts the scales plummet so it may be exact.

Thoth, the ibis-headed god of wisdom, stands to the right of the balance ever ready to record the verdict on his scribe's tablet.

In this particular case, Ani is found worthy to enter into the presence of Osiris. "His soul (ba) has stood in witness thereof. His case is exact on the Great Balance."

Note here that the soul (ba) is connected with the heart (ab).

Should Ani's heart not balance with "Truth," behind Thoth stands the monster, Am-mut, the "eater of the dead."

The god Horus then leads Ani into the presence of Osiris, who sits enthroned and attended by the goddesses Isis and Nephtys. Later scenes show Ani and his wife enjoying the delights and pleasures of the other world.

In similar representations, Osiris himself presides over the various proceedings.

The distinction between head and heart is one to which Carl G. Jung paid particular attention when he wrote:

> *The Pueblo Indians told me that all Americans are crazy, and of course I was somewhat astonished and asked them why. They said, "Well, they say they think in their heads. No sound man thinks in the head. 'We' think in the heart.*
>
> The Tavistock Lectures

In the Judeo-Christian teaching, there are found some 830 references to the heart in the King James version of the Bible, with 44 of these appearing in the New Testament alone.

Countless allusions to the various properties of the heart generally include the idea that it is the seat of the affections, desires, hopes and is symbolic of the spiritual nature of man. In the 16th century, Michel de Noble published a work in which he details, through a series of pictures, the various ill ends that can befall a heart when tempted by the mind and flesh. Classic is his depiction of the state of mortal sin as a heart occupied by a grinning devil!

It is St. Teresa who is most often connected with the heart in Christian art, while the flaming heart, a symbol of charity, is often associated with St. Augustine.

During the Middle Ages, the Order of The Bleeding Heart was established in honor of the Virgin Mary "whose heart was pierced with many sorrows."

Martin Luther often used the symbolism of the heart as well. A sermon for the consecration of the castle church in Wittenburg includes the following passage:

> *Christ must be sought with a heart... Such a request coming from the heart, God will grant... Thus He would have our hearts; and thus every feast of dedication should not merely be an outward consecration of a Church but rather a consecration of a heart unto God.*

By the Aztecs of Mexico, hearts were torn from the breasts of living prisoners, in order to be fed to the gods of the earth and sun.

The ancient Mayans cast hearts of living animals into fire as a sacrifice to the sun god.

Many primitive tribes have been known to eat the hearts of their enemies in order to acquire their courage.

An unusual belief held by an Indian tribe in the southern United States was that sickness meant that the victim's heart had been stolen by witchcraft. After battling with the invisible forces of evil, a symbolic heart made up from a stuffed ball of rags containing its own heart of grain would be recovered and fed to the sick person in order to recover.

Although the heart has been used for evil, generally it is held as a symbol of love. Hence, "to lose one's heart" means simply to fall in love.

A heart pierced by an arrow might be seen as symbolic of the female mystical anima being penetrated by the male phallus animus.

Thus, having hearts on Valentines is not just an accident, no more than is the belief that disappointment in love caused a "broken heart."

So strong is the belief that the heart truly represents the sum total of our spiritual existence that a practice arose during the 12th and 13th centuries of "heart burial."

Hearts of nobles, who happened to die abroad, were frequently brought back to their native land for burial, including those of Richard I, Henry I, Henry III, Edward I, and James II!

Robert Bruce, the famous King of Scotland, actually willed that his heart be entombed in the Church of The Holy Sepulchre in Jerusalem.

Children can often be heard voicing the great oath of secrecy, "Cross my heart and hope to die!"

According to the Doctrine of Signatures, during the Medieval Period heart-shaped plants were recommended for actual treatment of heart disease, including the wild pansy known as Heartease.

Certainly, a heart-to-heart conversation is without doubt the highest level of communication when looked at in this way.

Similarly, one who "wears his heart on his sleeve"

openly exposes his feelings to anyone and everyone with whom he comes into contact!

Among students of Metaphysical Bible interpretation, it has long been held that wherever the word heart appears in the Bible, what is really meant is the Unconscious Mind. Reflecting on this, Ernest Holmes, founder of Religious Science writes:

> *The heart is the center of Divine Love and perfect circulation. Its action is harmonious, vital, adequate and complete. There is no false action and no wrong action. The pulsations of life are steady, unceasing and perfect. "Let not your heart be troubled." Love is at the center of man's being, and the calm, continuous, pulsations of life are governed by Love.*
> SCIENCE OF MIND, p. 238

The Christian mystics, Harriette and F. Homer Curtiss, held similar views when they wrote:

> *The Spiritual Mind has its seat in the body at the Spiritual Heart, a secret point back of the breast, which corresponds to the physical heart; the heart being the seat of physical life and the Spiritual Heart being the seat of the spiritual life.*
> THE KEY TO THE UNIVERSE, p. 265

In yet another work, these authors pose the question:

> *For what good would the mystic fires of the seven-fold planetary Hierarchies be to man's spiritual unfoldment if there were*

not this spiritual Sun of Righteousness in
his heart occupying the central point or
throne of his being and able to respond to
the spiritual Hierarchies?
THE INNER RADIANCE, p. 287

Of especial interest to our current discussion of the esoteric significance of the heart are the words of the Old Testament prophet, Jeremiah:

The sin of Judah is written with a pen of
iron, and with the point of a diamond: it is
graven upon the table of their heart, and
upon the horns of your altars. (Jer. 17:8)

Commenting on this verse, the mystic and Biblical historian, Corinne Heline, writes:

Situated within the left ventricle of the
heart is the seed atom of the physical
body. This atom is indestructible and con-
tains a record of the ego's experience in a
body. After death of the dense body, from
this atom is taken the life record for purga-
torial and heaven-world experiences.
NEW AGE BIBLE INTER., p. 324

Returning, once again, to Patricia Hayes and, "THE GATEKEEPER" we find the following concurring statement:

The fourth energy point above the midsec-
tion is in the heart area and is the base of
your spiritual body or your soul. The heart
is a most important energy center for it
contains the awareness of love. That love

is both for your dimension and for the
spirit crystal, or God, within your spiritual
body. The radiation from the heart point
is spectacular, if you were to view it in
color. When it is activated and expressing
its level of awareness to the fullest, it is a
radiant shower of beauty. The energy is
intense, yet gentle and smooth.
Page 135

And so it is no wonder that both RoHun therapist and the client always come together during every session in the spirit of love.

Truly, it may be said that in so doing they "Dance Heart To Heart," which may be yet another reason why miracles of healing so commonly take place.

In the next chapter, we will examine yet another concept of great importance to the RoHun philosophy ... the chakras and subtle anatomy of man!

OK ... You don't have to read it tonight ... That is, unless you want to!

CHAPTER THREE

SEVEN GOLDEN CANDLESTICKS

And I turned to see the voice that spake with me. And being turned, I saw seven golden candlesticks; And in the midst of the seven candlesticks one like unto the Son of man, clothed with a garment down to the foot, and girt about the paps with a golden girdle.
Revelations 1:12-13

Already mentioned in an earlier chapter was the fact that the entire philosophy of RoHun, from its inception to the present, was given to Patricia Hayes by a spiritual entity who identified him self as Dr. RoHun.

In each communication, Patricia was simply advised what and how to do it, and to, "Please research this. You will find it most helpful in the healing process."

It is of great importance that this simple fact be kept continually in mind, for the process of RoHun as it currently exists is not the creation of Patricia Hayes, or anyone associated with her, but rather Dr. RoHun himself.

Every technique that is now used by RoHun therapists, worldwide, was suggested by Dr. RoHun and then subjected to vigorous research and proving before being accepted into the total program and philosophy.

Hence, in no way may RoHun be considered experimental and its clients guinea pigs.

"Experiential," ... definitely, "Yes!"

"Experimental," ... definitely, "No!"

Having clarified this very important point; we can now continue with our discussion. When Dr. RoHun first contacted Patricia, he gave her the following exercise, which served as a basis and clue to the further evolution of the therapy:

> *I have come to some conclusions that our staff wishes to share with you. I wish to give you a simple exercise that we have found valuable for removing the memory of illness... The brow chakra or the third eye is a most important energy point. This chakra has direct contact with all the levels of your awareness.*

Dr. RoHun then continued:

> *Your memories are stored within this chakra. The memory of pain and illness is a powerful one to alter. Pain and disease affect your physical, emotional, mental and spiritual bodies. We have worked with a group of souls in an experiment where we erased the memory of their illness by altering the rate of energy directly to the left of the center point of the brow chakra.*

To understand exactly what is meant by the word chakra we must now take a quick journey into the world of Yoga and Theosophy. I promise you it will not be boring!

A few years ago, if one were to mention the word yoga, a picture of a somewhat youthful contortionist, able to twist himself into various positions, would no doubt immediately come to mind.

In fact, even today, many think of yoga as merely yet another system of physical exercise, since it is often taught at the local "Y" or listed among various "adult education" courses offered in the evening at the high school!

Unfortunately, while this picture is indeed true, it is also greatly limited since it portrays only the physical or "Hatha" side of a greatly complex system of total self integration.

What is often forgotten is the fact that "Raja Yoga," the yoga of mental and spiritual development, is the most ancient system of the two.

Of this fact, Ramakrishna, one of the great modern sages of India (1833-86) wrote:

> The practice of Hatha Yoga will bring control over the body, but it will carry one only so far. Raja Yoga, on the contrary, deals with the mind and leads to spiritual results through discrimination, concentration and meditation ... A Raja Yogi seeks to realize the Universal Being. His object is to bring the finite human soul into communion with the infinite Spirit.

Hence, it can be said that all other yogas are only a preparation for the Royal Path or Raja!

The only reason we make mention of yoga, however, is that it contains in its teachings a most interesting and profound concept of what might best be called, "esoteric physiology."

In most mystical or occult systems found worldwide, there exists the belief in an invisible energy of some kind that radiates through, and permeates the entire physical body in spider-like strands.

For the yogis, where these strands of the subtle and physical bodies meet and interact, wheels or chakras are held to exist.

While these chakras have no physiological existence, they are thought to be focal points for the reception and transmission of energies, veritable psychic dynamos, vortices of force or energy.

According to psychics who have been gifted with the ability to actually see these centers, each center consists of three concentric whorls of energy (which rotate at various speeds) determined by the spiritual development of their possessor, and which constantly change both in color and rhythm.

Of these "Wheels of Fire," the theosophist Alice Bailey writes:

> *We must disabuse our minds of the idea that these centres are 'physical things.' They are whirlpools of force that swirl etheric, astral and mental matter into activity of some kind.*
>
> A TREATISE ON COSMIC FIRE

Not only can the various chakras reveal the state of one's physical health, but one's consciousness, personal spiritual development and vocational abilities as well.

In those undeveloped souls, the chakras are often seen as small in size, coarse in texture, dull in color and somewhat slow in movement.

The more responsive, more highly developed, sensitive souls will display chakras that are brighter in color, larger in size, finer in texture; and, always, possessing more rapid movement!

In almost all esoteric systems, the chakras are divided into major and minor bodies.

The major chakras are held to be seven in number, aligned vertically, parallel to the spinal cord, extending from the base of the spine to the very top of the head.

Although it is a matter of some dispute, most authorities number the minor chakras at twenty-one. In most persons, these are governed by the major chakras. Though, in some cases, where a major chakra has been inactive for some time, it may be necessary to treat these individually.

Confusion, also, sometimes arises as to the placement of the major chakras, due to various drawings made of these centers by psychic artists. These drawings often position the chakras "on the front of the body" instead of along the spinal column.

In actuality, while they are located approximately one inch above the dorsal surface of the spine, since they are energy and not matter, they can be "felt," by those sensitive enough, through to the front of the body as well.

Before we detail the significance of the seven major chakras as portrayed in the RoHun philosophy, perhaps we should make a few more general comments about these centers.

First, chakras always vary in intensity and size from person to person, depending on "who" and "what" they are.

For instance, a lecturer or singer might have larger throat and brow chakras than someone who might practice "mediumship." In the latter case, we would expect the solar plexus to be more developed.

Second, depending on whether a person is essentially a "head" or "heart" person, we might expect either the brow or heart center to be dominant!

Third, chakras ... even though they are "energy" based ... can be damaged; especially through sudden fear or shock. Likewise, continual worry, nagging or constant anxiety can actually interfere with their delicate balance.

Should a blockage occur at the energy entry point, psychological problems or endocrine dysfunctions can occur.

If this blockage occurs at the point of energy exit, the related endocrine gland will be over stimulated, thereby producing various physical illnesses.

Fourth, once damaged, chakras (as they are energy and not matter) can carry forward from lifetime to lifetime the "memory" of that injury, thereby producing a genetic inclination towards a particular illness or thinking pattern until the energy is correctly reprogrammed. In a sense, this is what RoHun actually does!

Fifth, each chakra has a connection with certain glands and organs of the body together with various states of consciousness. This is not to suggest, however, that the various chakras are the particular organs. For instance, the throat chakra is not the thyroid gland!

THE WHEELS OF LIFE

CHAKRA NAME:	ROOT MULADHARA	SPLEEN SWADHISTHANA	SOLAR PLEXUS MANIPURA
Meaning:	MULA: first, main ADHARA: support, foundation	SWA: your own ADHISTHANA: dwelling, origin, residence	MANI: jewel PURA: city
Quality:	Security	Creativity	Expansiveness Power Expression
Location:	Base of Spine Coccyx	Sacrum Pelvis	Lumbar, Naval, Solar Plexus
Endocrine Gland:	Adrenals	Gonads, Ovaries	Pancreas
Governs:	Spinal Column, Kidneys	Reproductive System	Stomach, Liver, Gall Bladder, Nervous System
Symbol:	Square/cross	Crescent moon	Triangle
Color:	Yellow	Orange	Red
Element:	Earth	Water	Fire
Foods:	Corn, Yams, Parsnips, Bananas, Lemons, Grapefruit, Honey-dew, Melons	Pumpkin, Carrots, Apricots, Cantaloupes, Peaches, Tangerines, Mangoes	Beetroot, Watercress, Spinach, Red Cabbage, Radishes, Red Plums, Black Cherries, Red Currants
Sense:	Smell	Taste	Sight
Ray*-	Fourth	Third	Sixth
Chemical Elements:	Carbon, Glucinum, Iridium, Magnesium, Molybdenum, Osmium, Palladium, Platinum, Rhodium, Ruthenium, Sodium, Tin, Tungsten	Aluminum, Antimony, Arsenic, Boron, Calcium, Copper, Helium, Selenium, Silicon, Xenon	Cadmium, Hydrogen, Krypton, Neon
Gemstone:	Coral	Pearl	Ruby
Planet:	Mars	Moon	Sun

THE WHEELS OF LIFE ... CONTINUED

CHAKRA NAME:	HEART ANAHATA	THROAT VISHUDDHA	BROW AJNA
Meaning:	That which is ever new	Pure amidst all purity	Command
Quality:	Love	Abundance, Space, Purity	Insight, Clarity
Location:	Between Shoulder Blades, Heart	Top of Back of Neck, Throat	Between Eyes, Center of Brow
Endocrine Gland:	Thymus	Thyroid	Pituitary
Governs:	Heart, Blood, Circulatory System, Vagus Nerve	Lungs, Bronchial/ Vocal System, Alimentary Canal	Nose, Ears, Nervous System, Lower Brain, 'Left' Eye
Symbol:	Circle	Oval	Third Eye
Color:	Violet	Indigo	Blue
Element:	Air	Space	Mind/Thought
Foods:	Purple Broccoli, Beet-tops, Purple Grapes, Blackberries	Blue & Violet Combined (Foods)	Most Blue Fruits; Blue plums, Blueberries, etc.
Sense:	Touch	Hearing	....
Ray*-	Second	Fifth	Seventh
Chemical Elements:	Actinium, Cobalt, Gallium, Niton	Bismuth, Ionium, Lead, Polonium	Caesium, Indium, Oxygen
Gemstone:	Sapphire	Diamond	Topaz
Planet:	Saturn	Venus	Jupiter

THE WHEELS OF LIFE ... CONCLUSION

CHAKRA NAME:	CROWN SAHASRARA
Meaning:	A thousand petals
Quality:	Higher Consciousness
Location:	Crown of the Head
Endocrine Gland:	Pineal
Governs:	Upper Brain, 'Right' Eye
Symbol:	Thousand Petal Lotus
Color:	Green
Element:	Consciousness, Self Realization
Foods:	Most Green Fruits and Vegetables.
Sense:	....
Ray*-	First
Chemical Elements:	Barium, Chlorine, Nitrogen, Radium, Tellurium
Gemstone:	Emerald
Planet:	Mercury

Above we have listed, in great detail, a summary of the correlation of the various chakras, according to the Yoga and Theosophical systems. Before we present to you now, in similar detail, the RoHun teachings in regard to the chakras, clarification must be made in regard to what is considered the second chakra.

In the Indian system presented above, you will note there is no mention of the "Spleen," which you will see plays an important role in the RoHun process.

The confusion regarding this center arises from the fact that it is not situated along the spinal column, as are the other centers, but rather lies to the left and above the naval, approximately at waist level.

Essentially, its function is to supply energy and vitality to all the other centers. This it does by channeling prana or life energy, drawn from the sun. Hence, any disturbance in this center will cause physical energy and vitality to lower in all, or any, of the other chakras!

Of this confusion, the late David V. Tansley, D.C. writes:

> There is another inaccuracy often seen in Western writings on the chakras, showing the spleen chakra as one of the major centres. This chakra, although of vital importance, is not counted as one of the major centres. Earlier authors, having included it, found it necessary to omit one of the other chakras in order to keep the number at seven. They left out the sacral chakra and attributed its action of vitalizing the reproductive system to the centre at the base of the spine, which, as we have seen, governs the kidneys and spinal column.
>
> RADIONICS & THE SUBTLE ANATOMY
> OF MAN, p. 31

For further clarification, later on in the same work, Dr. Tansley adds the following comments:

> Vitality is closely linked to the correct functioning of the spleen chakra, so it is necessary in any diagnosis of the chakras to determine the condition of this centre. Prana or vital force is distributed from the

spleen chakra to all of the other major chakras, and from there sent to the organic systems of the physical body.

In yet another section of this work, Tansley comments:

From the orthodox point of view the distinctive function of the spleen remains unknown. To the student of subtle anatomy it provides an interesting correspondence to the placenta and the umbilical cord, which connects the foetus to the mother for nutritional purposes. This cord, as we well know, is cut when the birth of the child is complete. Similarly the etheric silver cord is cut when the etheric and physical bodies are separated at death, and the inner man is "born" in full consciousness, into the world of a higher and more subtle dimension.

(Page 55)

Perhaps an easier way to avoid the confusion between the "Sacral" and "Spleen" chakras is simply to include and discuss both, which is essentially what is done by Shafica Karagulla, MD, and Dora van Gelder Kunz in their work, "THE CHAKRAS and the Human Energy Fields." (Theosophical Publishing House 1989)

The fact that we now have "eight" instead of "seven" chakras does not seem to disturb the authors of this excellent work!

Recognizing this same problem, Karagulla and Kunz write:

Descriptions of the chakras vary, and in some traditions the center located above the spleen is listed as one of the seven principal centers; in others, it is considered to be subsidiary. In DVK's observations, the spleen chakra is not perceived as a major chakra, but one which nevertheless plays an important role in the chakra system. (Editors Note: DVK can 'psychically see' the chakras!)... The spleen center is located at the left of the abdomen just below the tenth rib, and is connected with the spleen in the physical body.

Given this essential understanding as to what and where a chakra is, we can now proceed with a discussion of RoHun's conception of these various centers, which allow the RoHun therapist and client to perform what we have aptly called, "thought surgery!"

Before beginning this presentation, however, mention must again be made that the following ideas were channeled by Dr. RoHun, through Patricia Hayes, on various occasions.

According to Dr. RoHun, there are seven major thought patterns that each incarnated soul is affected by to some degree. These patterns lie within the etheric, emotional and mental bodies of man, thereby forming material consciousness.

As these thoughts are in essence "energy," they draw to their possessor similar thoughts in the universe, causing a continual repetition of that consciousness which bespeaks of frustration and limitation.

Because these thought patterns are so deeply ingrained in mankind's material consciousness, they can only be altered through the recognition of the soul, which is a higher energy, and by becoming spiritually aware.

As recognition and experience of the soul is internalized, which is what takes place during a RoHun session, the process of purification and reprogramming becomes a reality!

The Seven Major Faulty Thought Patterns are as follows:

1- I need "specific" material things and "specific" people to be happy. (**Root Chakra**)

2- I must worry and be anxious, or I will lose what I have, or not get what I want. (**Spleen Chakra**)

3- I cannot forgive others for what they did to me. I must hold on to my resentments, because that protects me from being hurt again. (**Spleen Chakra**)

4- I feel guilty and unworthy for all the times I've hurt others and made mistakes through wrong judgements. (**Solar Plexus**)

5- I must conform to what people think I should be, or I won't be accepted or recognized by them. (**Solar Plexus**)

6- People are to blame for my unhappiness. I must take control over others, so that I can have things as I want them, and not be taken advantage of or hurt. (**Solar Plexus**)

7- I must push people and situations for what I want. Love is a 'myth.' People take advantage of love! (**Solar Plexus**)

Take another long, hard look at this list.

Perhaps you can find your own faulty thoughts among these patterns.

If so, you would most likely benefit from RoHun yourself!

Also, please note that we have placed directly after each faulty thought pattern the specific chakra with which these thoughts commonly connect.

This does not mean that they may not be found in another chakra, but rather, based on many hours of experience and research, this is where they commonly reside.

Now, if you will, contrast the above with the following list which represents the major thought patterns of the spiritual man:

1- I have a kinship with all life. (**Crown Chakra**)

2- I feel free to expand to my full potential. There is purpose and direction in my life. (**Brow Chakra**)

3- I feel free to express my abilities as they unfold. (**Throat Chakra**)

4- I feel free to love and be loved. (**Heart Chakra**)

5- I feel confident about myself and my progress. (**Solar Plexus**)

6- I feel safe within my self and my purpose. (**Spleen**)

7- I feel good about myself and my progress. Life is to be enjoyed. (**Root Chakra**)

Surely, it is easy to see the difference between where most of us "are" and where we could be!

In the next chapter, Dr. RoHun will continue our discussion of the chakras by presenting his own views on this very important subject.

You may wish to "sleep" on what has been presented thus far. If so, sweet dreams!

CHAPTER FOUR

DR. ROHUN SPEAKS FOR HIMSELF!

Much as the unborn child floats in the embryonic fluid of the womb, so human beings are sustained by a sea of nourishing energies. The structure of the centers of force or chakras in the etheric, astral and mental vehicles remains constant throughout the lifetime of the individual, even while they are being continually replenished by the energies moving in and out from the three corresponding fields.
Karagulla & Kunz, THE CHAKRAS AND
THE HUMAN ENERGY FIELDS

"The Seven Chakras are important, because they represent the unfolding of man's development. Man can trace his stay on earth through the chakras and have vision of his true potential as a Man.

"The human race is in its young adulthood in its evolutionary progress. Primitive man, who used his creativity for survival, his sensual nature to satisfy his own sensual desires, and his brute strength to survive in the world, is a true picture of early man as a species. Man was perceiving his world through his 'Root' Chakra, the only chakra that was usable, or accessible to him, because of his sole emphasis on satisfying his needs.

"Each of the chakras represent a stage, or step, of man's increased perception. For example, the 'Solar Plexus' is where the majority of mass consciousness has evolved. The emphasis is on power, control and self-worth. The

'Spleen' Chakra, a holder of memories, assisted in the greater evolvement from survival and need to power and worth.

"The spleen, or digestive tract of experience, demonstrated to man that he could utilize his mind for greater achievement and worth.

"Man is at the threshold of another major step in the evolution of consciousness. Man is ready to take the next step to his 'Throat' Chakra, and become consciously aware of his capacity to express love. Man is reaching his arms high, and is asking for greater understanding of his nature. He has awakened his heart to help him know something better ... something more.

"RoHun Therapy assists him in his call for help. The discovery and recognition of his soul, through experiencing his thoughts and feelings, by means of the perception of his higher potential, or his higher centers, awakens his consciousness to another rung of the ladder of his evolution.

"The spiritual man steps forth through the expression of his soul. The term, spiritual man, does not imply any religious belief system, but rather an increase in perception to more wholistic thinking, expanded vision and intuitive understanding ... a greater expression of man.

"There are always the pioneers in every great age of man's leap upward. Those who, in their hearts, seek their greater self will have evidence of it. Man no longer desires to be a victim of self or another. Man desires to free himself of victimizing and of being a victim of a plastic world. He is seeking meaning to life, for the awakening of the 'heart' chakra has begun. Man is stirring to express all of his abilities, and his greatest inherent quality, love.

"RoHun Therapy was given to you (i.e., Patricia Hayes) through the perception of those in the spiritual world who are in touch with your world's desire for help. Man can achieve nothing more in the material world, until he opens his 'Throat' Chakra, through the assistance of his heart's desire.

"As the 'Throat' Chakra becomes conscious, and man perceives his ability to express love, all of his abilities and inherent qualities will be experienced in his reality. Man is demanding maturation. He knows, intuitively, that there is more to his potential than he is expressing.

"When man's 'higher' chakras (Heart, Throat, Brow and Crown Centers) are activated through RoHun Therapy, he makes the leap in consciousness that catapults him into greater perception, understanding and wisdom.

"The soul of man is born on the material plane. He instantly has conscious awareness of his spiritual origin and inherent abilities as a Son of God. In essence, he takes his rightful place and claims his inherent powers, which enable him to live a life of peace, happiness and abundance in this material world.

"He no longer feels the separation between himself and God.

"He is able to perceive the Whole as One and, each one as part of the Whole. He is able to relate his experiences, thoughts and feelings, through this expanded perception and, instantly understands the meaning and reasoning behind all his experiences.

"RoHun Therapy is a gift from our world to yours and a gift from your world to ours. As we help our brothers and sisters, we help ourselves; for we have a greater Whole, a greater One.

"Place your hand on your heart now and, speak through your heart to your soul. Whisper to yourself, 'Oh, my soul. I want to know you. If I awaken you, can I know greater life? Can I be greater than I am?'

"Wait until you feel a stirring motion or a tingling warmth, under your hand, and then again ask, 'Oh, my soul. Are you there? Can I truly perceive with greater vision?'

"Listen. Wait until you have heard an inner voice, which will move through you quietly, until you are aware of the answer. Then, persevere and ask again, 'Oh, my soul. I want to know more of you. Trust my intentions. What is the first step in knowing you better?'

"Listen for the impression, or symbol, that instinctively moves into your perception. You will either 'hear' with your inner ears or 'see' with your inner eyes.

"As consciousness evolves, man has use of more senses than his senses of sight, hearing, taste, touch and smell. His inner senses are awakened. His intuitive-creative nature dramatically increases. All of his five senses are increased. He is able to extend his seeing to more than surface appearances, his hearing to more than normal sounds, his touch to more than physical touch, his smell to more than physical odors, and his taste to more than ordinary tastes.

"He is able to extend his hearing, seeing, smelling, touching, and tasting beyond the norm of mass consciousness.

"This increases the understanding of his past and present experiences. It helps him direct and create the experience of love and harmony in his life.

"He begins to use his sense of vision to create an environment of beauty in his life. He begins to use his expression of love to create harmony in his life. He begins to use his sense of touch to create healing, in his life and others. He begins to use the sense of taste to discriminate what is good for him in relationship to the whole of his life. He begins to use the sense of smell to discern those things that he is to abstain from and to withdraw from his life.

"Man is on the threshold of maturation of all of his potentials and, most importantly, the expression of his true nature.

"RoHun is to be enjoyed and understood for what it is.

"RoHun is a 'process' that prepares and helps man to make the transformation to higher consciousness.

"RoHun awakens the consciousness to a higher level of evolutionary awareness."

DR. ROHUN
(Channeled Through Patricia Hayes)

Now that we have digested the good doctor's preliminary comments, we can share his unique understanding of the various Chakras as seen from the prospective of RoHun.

THE CHAKRA SYSTEM

#1 - The Root Chakra -
"How I See Myself"

Located at the base of the sacrum, the Root Chakra is the entrance of the body's force, and the seat of awareness of that life force's sustaining energy. This Chakra is the origin of sexual power. It is also the thrust of power that flows to stimulate all the cells in every part of the body.

The function of the Root Chakra is to influence sexual activity, regeneration, and creativity. This Chakra is concerned with basic security, survival, and existence. The purification and transformation of this Chakra enhances all forms of creative activity, personal growth, healing, intuition and intelligence. If it does not function properly, all the cells are eventually affected. The male and female energies should be balanced in this Chakra. The Root Chakra is full of experiences, particularly those of early childhood.

The RoHun therapist constantly returns to this Chakra to have the client do the RoHun exercise that stimulates the energy for RoHun therapy. This stimulates the energy, sending it up into the higher Chakras to be worked with. All people, situations, events, and negative emotions must be cleared out of the Root Chakra so that the energy going higher is clear, and the true self may generate the life force energy that sustains the body.

#2 - The Spleen Chakra - "How I Feel About Myself"

Located at the base of the spine, halfway between the pubis and the naval, is found the Spleen Chakra. The spleen is our desire body and our sexual activator and is closely associated with the Root Chakra. It is the assimilation center for all experiences found in the Root. It is the storage place for all experiences. The Spleen Chakra will retain the memory of 'all' major traumas from birth to the early twenties, particularly from the age seven to ten.

It is responsible for the memory of disease in the reproductive, digestive, and eliminative processes. If the thought patterns stored in this Chakra are faulty, health, behavior, and emotional response are affected. Its endocrine function is connected with the liver, pancreas, and spleen. It governs all the glands that influence metabolism, digestion, the detoxification of poisons, immunity to disease, and the balance of blood sugar.

This Chakra must be as thoroughly cleansed as possible during the first RoHun session, along with the Root Chakra.

It will need further cleansing in subsequent sessions, because of the layers of stored energies. It is most important for this Chakra to be cleansed, for the success of the continued therapy.

When working on this Chakra, pain may be felt in the heart, and a choking sensation may be felt in the throat as well.

#3 - The Solar Plexus -
"What I think About Myself"

Located at the base of the rib cage, just above the naval, the Solar Plexus is the power center, and the seat of self confidence. It is called the brain of material man. Faulty concepts and thoughts of power, and its misuse, are held within this Chakra. People and situations which have threatened the client's self esteem are found here. This center must be challenged, and the faulty thought patterns must be altered, as their cause is removed.

The time for thoroughly cleansing this Chakra depends on the individual. Some experiences are so traumatic that the client has removed himself from the experience, or has rejected it, covering the entire Chakra with a band of protection.

This band must be removed before the completion of the therapy.

Sometimes there are tentacles that hook into the Heart center, and pull toward the Solar Plexus. These tentacles must be cut. The client, in these cases, experiences love as power, and uses power to maintain a false sense of love and well-being. Occasionally, the client is operating solely from Solar Plexus energy, and has developed a strong energy current in this Chakra.

Once this Chakra has been cleansed, this power must be redirected, by drawing it up and out of the heart. Manipulation is transformed into harmonious giving and receiving, as the energy is drawn up into the Heart Chakra.

#4 - The Heart Chakra -
"How I Care About Myself"

Located in the center of the chest, the Heart Chakra is the seat of the feelings. It is the source of 'unconditional' love, compassion, spirit, consciousness, and every level of creation.

The heart is so vulnerable that traumas must be removed in layers. The heart is often protected by shields, belts, and other protective measures. A young, frightened self is frequently found in this Chakra, and must be removed.

The throat is directly related with the heart, as well as with the spleen. The client may experience choking, coughing, or crying as the shields are removed from the heart.

The Heart Chakra is the opening to the soul's expression, knowledge, and love. The spiritual body has its base in the Heart Chakra, and the client's insight is inspired with the cleansing of this Chakra.

#5 - The Throat Chakra -
"How I Express Myself"

The Throat Chakra is located at the top of the breastbone, and is the center for the expression of creativity, love, and abilities. It influences the thyroid gland, which affects the balance of the entire nervous system, metabolism, muscular control, and body heat production.

Since the throat is so closely connected to the Heart Chakra, this Chakra is often cleansed when the heart is cleansed. If not, the throat must be cleared of people and situations, and the client must be assisted to attune himself to the source of all energy. This Chakra expresses all of the soul's love and abilities as the Heart Chakra opens.

#6 - The Brow Chakra -
"How I Perceive Myself "

Also known as the 'Third Eye,' the Brow Chakra is located in the forehead indentation, just above the space between the eyes. It is the location of the spiritual mind.

It is not as cluttered as the lower Chakra, largely because the life force energy in this Chakra is dormant, for the most part.

The Brow Chakra influences the pineal gland, and relates to the pituitary gland, which is the master control center of the mind and body. It is the source of extrasensory perception (ESP), clairvoyance, clairaudience and clairsentience.

The cleansing and stimulation of this Chakra increases the energy that is brought up from the Root Chakra and it promotes communication between the left and right sides of the brain. Clairvoyance, clairaudience, and clairsentience are stimulated by the flow of this energy. Motivation for control of one's own life, and the release of others, is stimulated.

Judgment is removed by altering faulty thought patterns to provide for trusting that only those people and opportunities which can best allow the client to be his true self, will be attracted. The vision is stimulated. If the client has a physical illness, all memory of disease could be eliminated by working with the thought pattern, "Every molecule, cell, and atom in my body is working in perfect order and harmony."

#7 - The Crown Chakra - "How I Feel My Purpose"

The Crown Chakra is located at the top of the head. It does not need to be cleansed from trauma because the Divine Love, flowing through this Chakra, automatically cleanses it. It is a receiving station from the spiritual world.

The Crown Chakra influences the pineal gland, which is the seat of the Soul. The Crown Chakra is our tie with the universe and our kinship with all life. It is at this point that the soul attunes to its Source, and becomes one with the One, one with the Whole, and experiences the bliss, love and harmony of the One!

The Crown Chakra is activated by the therapist's asking that the divine energy flow through to attract all of those people and opportunities that will best allow the client to express 'his' or 'her' love, wisdom and abilities.

CHAPTER FIVE

THE SEVEN VISIONS OF SELF

Spiritually the 7 sacred planets constitute the 7 sacred centers in the body of the Grand or Heavenly Man, all receiving the life-force from His heart, just as physically they receive their life-force from the sun and send it forth again tinged with something of their own color and characteristic vibrations.

Harriet & Homer Curtiss,
THE KEY TO THE UNIVERSE, p. 223

Yet another way of looking at the Chakras is through what has been called, "The Seven Visions of Self," which are descriptive Names given to describe the action and interaction of the various chakras, after many years of research by RoHun therapists.

Each of us holds these Seven Visions of Self within our consciousness, which are strong images that impact our life energy and effect our health.

After a RoHun Therapist and client have completed the various purification techniques, which are parts and parcel of the early RoHun sessions, the therapist may elect to lead the client through these seven visions of self, in order to bring about still greater transformation.

As this is an advanced process in the total program, not everyone will be ready for it. But if one is, he or she can expect yet another RoHun miracle to take place.

While visiting Delphi, I asked Patricia Hayes to address this process, so that you and I might have a better understanding of its effectiveness and utility, as part of the total RoHun therapy.

What follows is Patricia's explanation in her own words:

"We do not see or envision ourselves in entirety. We tend to separate the aspects of our own being and identify with one or two of the aspects inclusively. Sages have always told us that we are multi-dimensional beings. That has had little meaning to us. In RoHun we have come to understand the aspects of Self and each of their functions. This new understanding makes it possible to begin to systemically unite each aspect as well as help each aspect to evolve awareness and purpose.

"There are Seven major aspects of our being. These aspects are found within our chakras, or energy centers, and like arms, legs, eyes and ears, each are responsible for different functions that assist us as a total being. When Socrates said, 'Know Thy self,' he was referring to the totality of Self, not just the body we see when we look in the mirror.

"Our Seven Selves make up our consciousness or, our whole being. Many individuals have not awakened their higher energy centers, or aspects of Self, and they lie dormant. They are living without the total potential of their whole being. It is most important to begin to know the aspects as well as awaken and utilize them. It is known that we use only 10 to 14% of our mind power. The rest of our potential lies within these chakras, energy centers or aspects of Self.

"Our RoHun research over the past years has provided a tremendous amount of knowledge and understanding of these aspects of Self. Having these seven major aspects within our total Self can be likened to having seven different 'persons' within us. Just because they're there does not mean they know each other, relate with each other, like, or cooperate with each other. And as I said, some may be sleeping and be totally unaware.

"The first aspect of Self is found in our Root Chakra. The function of this energy center is to provide us with our identity, or persona. In RoHun we have named the first root center, the PRESENCE. The PRESENCE holds the key to opening the door to know Self. If an individual's PRESENCE, or identity center, has no interest or inclination to know Self, or open its higher energy centers, little can be done. No one can do it for us. Each individual is responsible for his or her own evolution and personal growth. There is much healing that takes place with our self-identity, or Presence, during RoHun. One feels a new sense of self-confidence, worthiness, self-esteem and a sense of a loving presence.

"The next Chakra is the Spleen. We call this energy center 'The EMOTIONAL ONE.' It is our Magical Child within and reflects how we feel about ourselves. This Chakra has been called the garbage center because it is where we hold our resentments, guilt, and shame for everything that we have done wrong, including those things that people have done to us.

"Feelings of unworthiness block this Chakra. Many times we fear 'The EMOTIONAL ONE' and his or her erratic behavior. In the past, when we have followed our feelings, it has caused problems. Many times when we have felt it strongly, we have taken this feeling into the Root Chakra and sexual experience was the result.

"After awhile, a person begins to say 'I can't let my feelings rule me. I have to put them away. I've got to control myself.' So we have a society which has repressed its feelings. But this is a most important center. It is our Desire Body and our Astral energy. Through this center comes our joy, our vitality, health, excitement and intensity.

"We are not meant to live without joy. When the blocks are removed from this chakra, the kundalini, or life force, is free to flow upward to the higher chakras. Our feelings mature as we forgive ourself ... bringing intensity, joy and vitality to every other aspect of our being. The EMO-TIONAL ONE, when evolved, IS our healer! The energy of this chakra is powerful enough to bring cellular transformation to our physical form.

"The next chakra is the Solar Plexus. We call it 'The ACHIEVER' in RoHun. The function of this energy center is to accomplish. It has the ability to sustain 'doing' for long periods of time. It is also our center of personal power. If there are blocks, an individual will constantly attempt to prove himself or herself. For example, a person has a thought pattern, 'I must prove myself so that my parents will love me' or 'I must be a success so people will accept me.' There can also be blocks that cause the thinking, 'If I try, I will fail,' so the person never gets involved with what he desires to do.

"When people exclusively act from their ACHIEVER, they begin to believe that they are WHAT they do and lose sight of WHO they really are. They continue to 'do, do, do' until the body burns out and they become ill. In this case, they are no longer able to achieve so they drop down into their Spleen Chakra energy and find themselves miserable, unloved and experience a sense of 'feeling sorry for themselves.' Because the 'Inner Child' or 'Emotional One' has been repressed, and not allowed to enjoy life or have fun, this center is filled with negative feelings.

"These people force themselves to get better so they can get away from their negative feelings, and lift back up to The ACHIEVER, so they can get lost in 'doing' once again. The Solar Plexus, without the balance of the other energy centers, will work a person to death.

"In the advance process of transformation in RoHun, you are able to visualize each of the energy centers. You are able to see your thoughts, seeing exactly what you think of your Self in each of the functions. One man first saw his ACHIEVER as a huge growling bear. His thought about Self and achievement was, 'If I am to get anything done, I must be forceful, angry, powerful and make people fear me.' After the healing, he perceived a greater vision of Self. He saw a man of gentle strength with clarity and direction, who had a deep sense of caring, and who could accomplish easily and lovingly. He was able to see and experience himself as having love and concern rather than being 'self-centered' in the importance of 'achievement' exclusively. Many of our 'control' and 'helpless' issues come from this energy center. The leap in consciousness that is happening in the 'New Age' or 'Inner Age,' as I like to call it, is the leap from the Solar Plexus to the next energy center or the Heart Chakra. Our Heart Chakra is the center of our Being; the mediator between the three lower energy centers and the three higher energy centers.

"Within the Heart Chakra lies our Divine consciousness. We call this center 'The ONE WHO CARES.' This is the only center we have that naturally knows unconditional love and is able to facilitate healing through total acceptance and Love. The potential of unconditional love lies deep within this chakra and is often covered with layers of protection. So often, when an individual is hurt in love relations, he or she places walls of protection around this chakra forming the thoughts, 'If I love I will get hurt!' or 'There is suffering connected with love.'

"He or she protects him or herself from love rather than allowing his or her love to flow freely outward into our world. This is faulty thinking and keeps people from attracting the love and positive experiences they are capable of experiencing.

"This faulty thinking stems from 'traumatic experiences.' Because the higher Brow Chakra of wisdom and perspective is not functioning yet. These people perceive the hurtful personal experience of love as 'abandonment' or 'betrayal' by another person, blaming the other person and adopting an attitude of 'not trusting' any relationship. They close the Heart Chakra tighter and also their potential for truly loving. This problem affects the majority of individuals at one time or another ... so let me shed some light on 'why' and 'how' this happens.

"Again, faulty thinking and lack of self knowledge perpetuates the problem. For example, imagine for a moment that you are at a party with many people. You see someone of the opposite sex on the other side of the room. This someone is beautifully and physically attractive. You want to meet this person. (Remember the Desire Body, i.e. the spleen is very powerful.) You turn up your charm and somehow make your way over to meet them. Your Desire Body falls in love with this person. Before you know it, you are involved in a relationship or marriage. Three or five months, or years later, you wonder 'what' happened. Several things happened...

> You turned up your charm to get what you wanted (**Spleen Chakra**).
> You caught the person up in your magnetic aura (or energy field) which lifted his or her energy (**Spleen Chakra**).
> Neither of you could sustain the charm or vital interest so you returned to your normal energy (**Solar Plexus**).
> Perhaps there was never the unconditional love for the whole person (**Heart Chakra**) that is necessary to sustain a loving 'heart to heart' relationship.

> These can be the results:
> The relationship continues because of 'duty,' 'convenience,' 'children,' or 'security.'
> Feelings of resentment, hostility, entrapment and loss of vital energy can occur.
> Divorce or separation.
> The thought, 'I will never give myself to someone again.'

"This relationship began from intentions other than love, such as passion, and a desire to get what you wanted. If the higher chakras had been functioning, you may have perceived the attractive person from across the room in a different way. Your thoughts may have sounded like this: 'That is an attractive person' OR 'They look very interesting but I can feel that they are not sensitive, or ready for an in-depth relationship. I'll admire them from a distance. I must have someone who can be true to me and who is able to truly love and give affection.'

"The perception of the higher chakras simply evaluates through the interpretation of energy 'where' a person is. This is done without judgement. You can converse with the person lovingly, but will not get intimately involved expecting the person to be something that isn't possible.

"Your wisdom and love of Self directs your desire towards positive and fulfilling experiences, rather than experiences that cause you to feel unworthy, helpless and a victim.

"Our treasure and abundance lie within our Heart Chakra. We must begin to move through the protective layers and find 'the essence' of our true potential. We don't believe in our ability for unconditional love because we have made so many mistakes in our lives. But we have learned from our mistakes; they have been learning experiences.

"Our faulty thoughts, fears and desires have attracted our negative experiences, not our love and wisdom. When we unlock our heart and let our rich abundance of loving thoughts and feelings flow outward into the universe, we automatically begin to open the higher centers of expression, vision and purpose.

"We begin to attract people who are capable of loving. We attract work situations where we can love our work, rather than working out of duty. We invite self growth and understanding and begin the journey toward wholeness by discovering our true potential as a human being of luminosity.

"The Throat Chakra in RoHun is called 'The EX-PRESSER.' Its function is to express our abilities and potential. If there are blocks, the expression is held back and a tightness occurs. For example, if your feelings are negative and resentful, you may have to control your expression so you don't hurt others.

"A male executive came to me because he had difficulty expressing himself in his work. He was a vice president for a Fortune 500 company. He said it was painful for him to speak at meetings. He wanted to overcome this.

"When we began working on his Throat Chakra and he saw his EXPRESSER, he was frightened. His EXPRESSER was a 'devil.' Basically he thought his EXPRESSER was evil. This thought came from a past experience where he misused his expression. He was still identifying with this past experience.

"He looked at the negative experience, forgave himself, and his EXPRESSER changed to a little girl who was crying. His ONE WHO CARES went to the girl and held and loved her. The little girl changed to a mature man with loving eyes and a desire to share what he knew.

"The healing had taken place. The man grasped a greater vision of Self. Because his thoughts of Self were transformed, he was now able to express himself at meetings.

"This sounds too simple, but healing IS simple when you begin to know your greater Self and learn how to access it. We are limited because of ignorance of the Self. While our society teaches us about our physical and material world, our academic institutions place no value on inner or self knowledge, for which there is a great need. This is why you see so many 'New Age' organizations all over the country. These new places of learning teach the value of 'Knowing Self.'

"The Brow Chakra or 'Third Eye' is called The VISION-ARY. The function of this energy center is perception and vision. If the life force is flowing to activate this center, we have the ability to objectively view a situation. We can see the big picture.

"If this center is blocked, our vision and judgement are shut down. When blocked, we are constantly judging self and everyone else around us. Even if we do ten things perfectly, and then make a mistake on the eleventh, we judge ourselves and feel unworthy.

"The Brow Chakra is our psychic center. We see people who have developed the Brow Chakra but have not healed or integrated the other chakras. Thus, we have many people with wonderful ideas but who can't accomplish their visions. The ACHIEVER is dormant and not cooperating with the VISIONARY.

"The secret of RoHun is not only to activate all the energy centers, but also to bring all the aspects of Self into a state of cooperation. Now we have the Whole Self, or total being, living and expressing. Each is concerned about the greater good of the whole.

"There are many abilities we have developed in past lives that we can utilize in this one. Because our conscious-ness continues after the death of our physical body, our thoughts continue to attract experiences which will confirm them. We can access these abilities and express them along with our present talents.

"For example, a stewardess with no apparent writing ability connected with a past life in which she was a writer. This experience inspired her to write four books, an off-Broadway play and create a game which has just been published. Needless to say, she is not a stewardess any-more even though she enjoyed her work! She now enjoys being acknowledged as a writer, sharing her feelings and thoughts with thousands of people.

"Our consciousness is 'Us.' You might liken it to a huge bubble that encloses our thoughts and feelings. Our physi-cal body is the outlet for 'Us.' It is the vehicle of expression. Our PRESENCE is responsible for getting in touch with who we are, our continued growth, and the sharing of our love and wisdom. Without the interest or cooperation of our PRESENCE (Root Chakra), we cannot tap into that mag-nificent Being which we are. We cannot recall our Soul's history, bringing understanding to our present life.

"The next chakra is the Crown. The Crown is called the Inspirer and the function of this energy center is PURPOSE. When this center is activated we feel purpose in our life. We feel connected and have a kinship to all life. We know we have existed BEFORE and will continue to exist after the death of our physical body, because we are consciousness, not just form.

"We see the pattern of our evolution. We feel connected to our source and know we are an aspect of God 'Becom-ing.'

"There is a synchronicity between physical happenings and spiritual understanding. This center is not often blocked, but many times it is inactive, because no energy flows upward to it. As the life force is freed to flow upward to our Crown, we begin to sense that we have a purpose in this lifetime, and begin to explore our spiritual memory to find out what it is.

"Without integration, we feel at war with ourselves. For

example, have you ever wanted to go on a diet to lose weight? Your ACHIEVER has convinced you that you must do this for your health and happiness. As your ACHIEVER is expounding this plan, your EMOTIONAL ONE reaches into the refrigerator and gobbles a 'goody.'

"Also a person can open the higher chakras and still be blocked in the lower ones. This person may feel purpose and experience spiritual vision but may not be able to achieve.

"We call these people 'top heavy.' They have escaped from the world and many times have difficulty relating to people.

"We are not meant to escape our world by living only in our higher chakras. We are whole beings. Heaven is not a reward of a future world if we are good. Heaven is a state of being, a kinship with all life wherever we are. Knowing our 'Godness' (goodness) and creating from that conscious-ness is heaven. A state of hell comes from identifying with an 'isolated self' and seeking power and control to fill the emptiness of an 'unworthy self.'

"Our seven chakras are the psychic organs and limbs of our body. Balance and integration of Being ARE possible which is the purpose of RoHun. By understanding the evolution of the Seven Selves, we have a system of enlightenment for the first time. In the purification stage of RoHun, the objective is to clear the blocks from each chakra, allowing the energy to flow powerfully from the Root to the Crown.

"In the advanced stage of RoHun, the objective is transformation. This is accomplished through an alchemi-cal change of energy within each chakra. The energy of the lower chakras moves to the Heart Center and then unites with the higher chakras.

The ONE WHO CARES (Heart Chakra) works with and through the energies of:

The PRESENCE (Identity)
The EMOTIONAL ONE (Vitality of healing)
The ACHIEVER (Accomplisher)
The EXPRESSER (Free expression of abilities)
The VISIONARY (Insight, perception and wisdom)
The INSPIRER (Purpose and direction)

"Now one is able to enter into relationships, work and live life on a day-to-day basis with purpose, clarity, freedom of expression, love, confidence, vitality ... all with a sense of personal power to positively affect his or her life and the world.

The ONE WHO CARES (Heart) has a board of directors that is working for the greater good of all the chakras. For example, when I go to work, I feel the PURPOSE in what I am doing. My VISIONARY is with me providing the insight and clarity necessary. My EXPRESSER expresses freely. I care deeply about my work and purpose. Opportunities are always being attracted so that my ACHIEVER can accomplish my purpose.

"Best of all, there is always a creative flow of vitality and enjoyment in what I choose to do.

The power of RoHun heals the insecurities of:

1. Looking to others to prove self.
2. Seeking approval of others to accept self.
3. Searching for things and people to make you happy.

4. Wondering what you could be doing to achieve.
5. Being a victim.
6. Feeling unworthy or resentful.
7. Blaming others.

"We, as human beings of luminosity, have so much more potential than we are using. Ignorance keeps us blinded. Attachment keeps us bound.

"The RoHun therapist is a Master Teacher in a sense, directing you to your higher abilities, unblocking your natural force of energy, and allowing you to experience the 'goodness' and Power of your loving being.

"The RoHun Therapist dances heart to heart with you in your becoming a whole being.

In other words ... RoHun is a journey to Wholeness!"

CHAPTER SIX

THE NEGATIVE SELVES

The importance of the seven plexii in any system of medicine, Eastern or Western, has not still been recognized or appreciated. It is indeed regrettable. The seven plexii are the seven power centres in the human body through which cosmic forces function during the life time of a person.
Dr. B. Bhattacharyya, GEM THERAPY

There yet remains one other way in which to look at these chakras, namely, through the eyes of what Carl. G. Jung called the 'shadow.'

In RoHun, at least four dark horses have been recognized and saddled. Let us now discuss them one by one.

THE UNWORTHY SELF

Located in the Root, Spleen and Heart Chakras, particularly, but influencing all other chakras as well, the 'Unworthy Self' dates from the earliest recollection. Perceiving itself not loved, it concludes it is unlovable. Fears of abandonment are the result, leading to the "getting-keeping-controlling" thought patterns that reinforce the lack of success and abundance, thereby preventing the ability to receive love. This self is expressed in thoughts like:

I don't deserve love.
I don't deserve success.
I couldn't have done...

I can't let you know me, because if you did
you couldn't love me!
If my own mother couldn't love me, who
could possibly love me?
I must be awful for that to have happened.
If you say you love me, you must want
something.
What's wrong with you that you would love
me?

To return this self to the light, the RoHun therapist
assists the client to acknowledge, and then forgive and love
this Unworthy Self, by releasing it into the light, where it can
be safe, grow and know love.

THE FRIGHTENED SELF

Located principally in the Spleen, but strong in the Solar
Plexus and the Heart, the Frightened Self is helpless, full of
doubt, anxiety and tension. It is caged, not free to express
or be who he or she is.

Feeling unworthy, it is afraid it will be abandoned and
won't be taken care of.

The Frightened Self is fragile.

Its thoughts are expressed in terms like:

I don't know if I can love or have what I want.
I feel insecure.
Nobody can get close to me.
I'm afraid to get close to anyone.
I am afraid that no one can or will love me!

Here the RoHun therapist's task is to send the Frightened Self up to the light, so it can find illumination, awareness and teachers to help it.

It must be sent safely, so it can evolve.

"Hug it and love it. Forgive it and forgive yourself for whatever."

The therapist's job is to help the client realize that light is the safest place for the Frightened Self, and that it is the ONLY place for it to grow!

THE HELPLESS SELF

Located primarily in the Solar Plexus, but with a strong influence on all the other chakras as well, the Helpless Self feels powerless and/or controlled, and compensates by overpowering, or manipulating, whenever possible.

The Helpless Self is limited, without options, trapped in either helplessness or controlling others.

The Helpless Self is a victim of people and situations.

The Helpless Self's thoughts are expressed in terms like:

> I can't do it myself.
> I can't make it happen.
> I need someone to take care of me.
> If you don't do what I want you to do, I will nag
> you until you do!
> I feel as if my life is out of control.
> I don't have a chance of success.
> My children will take care of me when I am old
> and feeble.
> I must have eight hour's sleep, or I am a
> wreck!

THE JUDGE

Located in the Brow, the Judge is the Self that "rules" that the client is unworthy, frightened and helpless.

Here is where the intent of the client is located.

The Judge feels it is necessary to keep everyone in line, his Self included! He directs attention to every little thing he can find that is wrong. He sets himself up both as God and as teacher.

No one loves him; for he has no mercy, compassion or forgiveness.

Most of all, he is unable to feel or give loving feelings.

The Judge separates from the greater self of others, by reminding everyone where they have failed or are wrong, and from the Greater Self of the Cosmos for the same reasons.

The Judge has the most prominent position in the Hierarchy of Selves. No wonder he is the most difficult to forgive and release.

Letting go is the single most difficult task for human beings to accomplish. Letting go of the Judge could mean letting go of our discernment and our feelings of being conscientious.

If we send the Judge to the light, who would replace him?

How would we control ourselves if the Judge is forever exiled?

Some think the Judge is their conscience, and so they protect him.

The Judge MUST go in order for the client to be free.

It is most important to understand that as RoHun progresses, and the "lower" chakras are cleansed of faulty thought patterns, the energy consistently lifts and activates the 'higher' chakras.

As the Heart, Throat, Brow and Crown are stimulated, the higher consciousness is activated. Creative, intuitive and spiritual energies are put into motion, and the client becomes spiritually active.

The spiritual guidance system, within our higher consciousness, replaces the Judge with a higher quality of discernment. This quality is evaluation.

Evaluation is a simple discerning ability that allows one to have clear perception of where one is.

Judgment, on the other hand, is a separating disability that causes distance and isolation, and distorts clear perception.

When one judges, one is unable to allow the healing love to connect with others.

When one evaluates, the healing love is directed to the area of another's needs!

This Judge expresses in terms such as:

> You didn't do it right!
> You have to be right.
> Forget understanding; you've go to have
>   justice.
> He's wrong.
> I'm wrong.
> I'm a victim.
> They are bad.
> They are inferior.

I am inferior.
I don't have enough.
I must show them what to do, because they
    will do it wrong!

When the RoHun therapist and client understand the reasonings in letting go of the Judge, the forgiving and releasing process has a long-lasting effect.

The client no longer fears losing control of his or her life.

The caring and loving qualities of the Higher Self are able to help the client connect, consistently, with his or her own inner resources and those of others.

As you get rid of the other three Selves, the Judge won't have as much to do.

Hence, it will be much easier to get rid of him! To assist in this process, the RoHun therapist instructs the client as follows:

> I want you to imagine yourself going into your head and stretching your self! You can now trust your feelings. You don't need a Judge. Give the Judge a break. Give him a vacation. You once needed him, but now you are more aware and don't need him. Give him a hug and let him go. Free him to go into the light and learn of love.

Now the Judge can be replaced with the Helpful Evaluator, a self that provides facts and discrimination without the hurtful value judgments of the Judge!

Once the Judge is taken off the bench of criticizing power, higher consciousness is able to simply evaluate and encourage, and to praise the steps of progress already made, no matter how small or large they might be.

Love, and appreciation of Self, perpetuate the continued spiralling motion of Self Realization, and Self-Unfoldment, of our true Divine Natures.

While the above selves represent the four most commonly found Debilitating Selves, others will no doubt continue to emerge with continued RoHun research. In fact, an additional five Selves have already raised their voices ... The Angry Self ... The Suffering Self ... The Phony Self ... The Dutiful Self and the Resistant Self!

We leave a discussion of these to another time and place.

In the next chapter, we turn our attention to a most important topic ... The marriage of RoHun and Psychiatry!

CHAPTER SEVEN

A PSYCHIATRIST GOES CRAZY OVER ROHUN

These centers, each with its 7 subsidiary centers, are sometimes called the '49 crucified saviors,' signifying that the vital power of these centers is at present misused and crucified, and ere they become man's Saviors they must be resurrected from the tomb of matter and made to function in a higher state. They are called the '49 fires' because their light guides man to Superman.

Homer & Harriette Curtiss,
THE VOICE OF ISIS, p. 165

Nicholas Demetry, M.D., is a graduate of the Emory University School of Medicine. He received his postgraduate training in psychiatry, specializing in trans-cultural aspects of psychiatric care, from the University of Hawaii. For the past eight years he has been working in the fields of psychiatry and holistic medicine.

He is a member of the American Medical Association and the American Holistic Medical Association, and has travelled extensively, studying a variety of natural therapeutic approaches to health care.

He has incorporated his traditional training, his understanding of personal transformation and the natural healing process into an integrated preventive medical practice.

Dr. Demetry also serves as a current director of the RoHun Institute, a position he shares with Patricia Hayes and Marshall Smith.

I had the wonderful opportunity to chat briefly with him about his involvement with, and dedication to, RoHun while I was visiting Delphi.

What follows is our most interesting conversation:

ZOLAR

How did you feel when you first discovered RoHun?

NICHOLAS

I guess it was a feast for me. It was an absolute feast, a smorgasbord, totally. It really was!

For instance, one of the beautiful things I had to address with clients before RoHun, which was always a problem, was the death and dying issue, as Kubler-Ross talks about.

How should I deal with it with people?

In RoHun I had a number of patients who had loved ones who were departed, for instance, grandparents. Maybe their only source of love in their family, usually an abusive one, was this grandparent.

We would go into the RoHun session and ask that "departed" loved one to come back and dialogue with us. Often we would reach a healing completion. I saw tremendous things.

One lady I had was holding her grandfather so tightly to herself; feeling guilty about his death for not being there at the time he passed over. She was his only loved one and vice-versa.

We came to find out that her grandfather was doing very well on the other side. What she was feeling was his concern for her that she wasn't doing very well with her life.

Eventually, she came to a resolution about this, let him go, and allowed new changes to come into her life!

ZOLAR

When you did this, did you actually believe you were bringing this entity back?

NICHOLAS

Initially, with a left brain bias, in a Jungian perspective, you might say you are bringing a lost or split fragment of the psyche back to that person to integrate. That's certainly correct, I feel.

At the same time, if you are looking at it in a right brain perspective, you go beyond that thought and become more metaphysical and spiritual and say you are 'actually' attracting that person to you!

Actually, they have never left!

They are right here all along.

There were three areas I incorporated into my practice, as a busy psychiatrist and clinician, after my exposure to RoHun. I did not always have time to sit back. I was seeing eight or nine patients a day, five days a week.

Before I worked with RoHun, I always had a problem wondering how I was going to clear myself of all the psychic stuff that came to me.

I would sit in that chair, being receptive, and "ahaing" people, and would go home and feel like a monster.

I would have to go out and jog, and swim, and do all kinds of things I could.

RoHun, being a directive process as it is, I was able to work with its energy. I knew that it is was a transformation process, that people didn't get stuck. They didn't go away feeling worse than when they came in, as they often do in regular therapy, and have one little breakthrough every six months.

They got out of there; they came to resolutions.

This was very satisfying to me.

ZOLAR

In how 'many' sessions were you seeing resolutions?

NICHOLAS

I worked in three ways. First, I had clients that were fairly healthy ... who in psychiatric terminology we would say had adjustment reactions ... neurotic depression, addictive type problems, alcohol-drug abuse ... but who were more amenable to supportive therapy, or therapy per se.

In RoHun, the length of their therapy was shortened considerably. Their ability to access the more positive, life-affirming quality was greater. They got away from thinking of themselves as being ill and looking for wholeness.

Then I began to see that the aim of RoHun was really healing and wholeness, not just perpetuating psychopathology, and their identity in that, their sick role!

ZOLAR

Except that the 'wholeness' was not just what we would call physical?

NICHOLAS

That's right. It's physical, mental, emotional, spiritual ... a total wholeness.

ZOLAR

It's like "One Stop Shopping!"

NICHOLAS

Right. Exactly. That's it!

So I had some clients that were in the ball-park where they could go through short term psychotherapy at that point.

They went through three, four, five RoHun sessions.

They cleared through their major issues.

Now I had some of my associates come to me and say, "No one clears through their issues in just three, four or five sessions!"

But the truth of it is that if a person is ready, and motivated, and this is the appropriate therapy for them, it will work in that fast a fashion!

ZOLAR

Are you saying that somehow you attracted people for whom this was an appropriate therapy? Is RoHun of such a nature that it is an appropriate therapy for everybody?

NICHOLAS

I feel that RoHun could be appropriate for anyone.

The spectrum I worked in was that I had people who were healthy coming to me, who had never seen a psychiatrist before in their life. They would come in and say, "You know, this is a historical moment for me. I never thought I would see a shrink, but here I am."

These people, who were healthy, were looking for self growth. They were looking for enlightenment, for reduction of stress in their lives, enhancing their relationships, their capacity to have more happiness in their lives.

They wanted to access their creativity more, to release faulty thought patterns, past guilts, things that were still nagging at them.

Many of these people would come to me, and within a short term, they would do wonderfully.

I soon did RoHun on a lot of my family, my friends. These were basically healthy people, considered normal in society. They all benefited!

ZOLAR

Did you use this process on your wife?

NICHOLAS

Yes. I used this on her and she benefited, too!

ZOLAR

Do you think that RoHun can be used by one family member on another?

NICHOLAS

Yes. I think it is a little easier to do than if you were just a traditional psychotherapist, because you get to things quicker, and you can work them out. However, if you share a mutual issue; of course, it is going to be a little more difficult.

ZOLAR

What happens when the RoHun therapist does share the same issue as the client?

NICHOLAS

Then what happens is that you have someone reflecting you.

Two things can happen:

> If you have a lot invested in hiding or repressing that in yourself; you won't allow the client to have an unfoldment of healing.
> If your intent is to heal it in yourself as well, then a mutual healing can actually take place!

ZOLAR

You don't run into the same kind of block that traditional therapists have when this happens?

NICHOLAS

The transference counter/transference reactions are generally minimal in RoHun. There may be a little something that comes up, but usually it is minimal.

ZOLAR

How do you explain this? Why is it?

NICHOLAS

I think that, on the one hand, you are not dealing directly with the personality level of things so exclusively.

There is always a "spiritual dimension" involved.

More important than anything is the fact that, in RoHun, there is a tremendous incentive to allow unconditional love to be present.

This unconditional love has an uncanny way of setting everything in its proper place, so that's why I can say it!

When you deal strictly on the ego level, as you often do in ego oriented therapies, there is always this exchange going on, unconsciously, between client and therapist, because there is not an acknowledgment of that level.

A fascinating thing happens when you go into RoHun, you go directly to the unconscious.

In the trance state, I have often seen RoHun being what I would call a "lucid" or "waking dream."

Here the client is experiencing the dream, but very lucidly and very aware. At the same time he has a helper or facilitator, who's there by his side, and acts as his support in healing.

And as they both go through the healing, they are both accessing the unconscious and conscious minds "simultaneously."

ZOLAR

This is a most unusual occurrence, is it not?

NICHOLAS

Very unusual!

ZOLAR

There are no other therapies that do this?

NICHOLAS

No others. There are some therapies out now that work ... for instance, the holotrophic breath work. There are some others coming out that do work with the unconscious to bring stuff up, but that simultaneousness is not available.

ZOLAR

That is a very brilliant observation. It didn't occur to me.

NICHOLAS

This is very important and very powerful.

The Jungians talk about bridging the Ego, Self, and the axis between the Ego and Self. I don't see any other way to truly bridge it than through love and healing, unless you have a simultaneous awareness.

ZOLAR

The Jungians are stuck with dreams. If they don't get the dream material, they have nothing to work with.

NICHOLAS

Yes. And it's after-the-fact. It's not simultaneous.

ZOLAR

It's also not spontaneous, and it's not 'Now.' It's not contemporary.

NICHOLAS

Exactly!

ZOLAR

Depending on when the session is scheduled the dream could have occurred as much as a week ago. By now, certainly stale!

NICHOLAS

Clients have often shared it this way.

They say, "It's as if I am in the audience looking at my life on the stage, and I am on the stage enacting it! And there is a Director, who I call Therapist, who is off to the side, and with whom I am conferring and co-directing."

This seems to describe RoHun really well.

ZOLAR

Do you think, because of the revolutionary ideas in RoHun, that it only belongs in the hands of the trained therapist? Do you think there is room for lay analysts as well?

NICHOLAS

I think there is room for both. I really do.

I have seen trained therapists come through the RoHun training; I have seen lay people come through.

I think the advantage the trained therapist will have, of course, is having dealt therapeutically with people for many years. They know the parameters. They know all the extremes, so it might make it a little easier for them to know where to go with things.

ZOLAR

Wouldn't it also make it more difficult, since they would have to 'unlearn' certain things?

NICHOLAS

That is also true.

ZOLAR

Do you see the possibility of the school eventually having two levels of programs? A program just for health care professionals, and one for laypersons?

NICHOLAS

I would like to see that developed. Patricia and I have talked a lot about this. I think it would be really great.

Putting this in the hands of skilled therapists, who are open and ready to go on; it's a tremendous tool!

ZOLAR

Is RoHun a therapy or a process?

NICHOLAS

I think from my own perspective as a psychiatrist; I see it as a therapy process!

ZOLAR

You've upstaged me. You combined the two!

NICHOLAS

You're right. Also, for the therapists, I feel it can be a tremendous tool, in so far as what I've often done with people who are more severely disabled, who have personality disorders.

Schizophrenia, I don't touch. They cannot integrate as there is no ego strength.

People, who are more mainline, I am talking about. I might do some talk therapy with them, because they may need this.

And when something key comes up ... around anger, around grief ... something they need to release emotionally, and get a deeper understanding of, I put them on the table for a RoHun session.

I 'key' in and do that session on them, and it breaks the blockage. After, I bring them back and we continue our talk. When the time is right, we go in for another one.

Also, there is something else which is very exciting with RoHun. I work at a wholistic center with homeopaths and other practitioners. I find that RoHun is a tremendous adjunct when people have physical illness. There is something about the chakra clearing.

In fact, there are some biological medicine physicians in Germany now, working on chakra homeopathies.

Particularly, we find in emotionally based illnesses, or stress related illnesses ... such as colitis, diabetes, right down the line ... all these things are very amenable when worked with physical therapy and RoHun.

ZOLAR

Have you seen any physical healing from just RoHun alone?

NICHOLAS

Yes. I think the primary area is with diabetes, which has been phenomenal. We have had one client, a woman who had juvenile onset diabetes, and who was on about 70 units of insulin. She was 35-36 years old when she came to us, which was early in our work with physical illness.

I did a RoHun session with her, and she had an issue that came up about her father leaving her, at the onset of the illness. There was much grief around her. She also had issues with her mother, surrounding control.

In her session, I had to do something creative I had

never done before. I put two eyes on her pancreas, had her envision it and talk to it, to get in touch with the grief inside it, and then to dialogue with the tissue to release the energy. The next day when she tried to take her normal amount of insulin, she had a reaction. So she decided, on her own, that she would cut it down.

She cut it down about 15 points, with no problem at all!

After several other RoHun sessions, she continued to reduce it.

She is now down to virtually 'no' insulin at all!

ZOLAR

That is certainly incredible!

NICHOLAS

It is. Now this has been repeated at least two other times I know of, with other therapists.

ZOLAR

Do you think it is possible, then, at some point to get a controlled study of this?

NICHOLAS

I would love to do a controlled study of this. It says something to us about illness, not only being physically-based, but having an emotional cause as well.

ZOLAR

I always thought that diabetes was a replacement for a lack of love ... a sweetening of the blood ... a sweetness one did not get in life!

NICHOLAS

Exactly.

ZOLAR

It is interesting that on such a simplistic level one might find this truth. This is extraordinary.

NICHOLAS

I agree.

ZOLAR

I know you are on the Board of Directors of the RoHun Institute here. Where do you see the whole thing going?

NICHOLAS

Well, I feel that in a Jungian sense the Collective Unconscious is ready for RoHun. By the looks of it, in the last few months with the Japanese coming over, and the interest that has been shown, everyone I talk to seems to know something about RoHun.

I think there is a tremendous future in it.

You know there are therapies that come up for each Age!

Gestalt came up in the 70's, Fritz Perls was big at Esalan, and then you had other things come in after that.

I think RoHun is the therapy of the future!

ZOLAR

Because it's an energy therapy!

NICHOLAS

Yes.

ZOLAR

The medicine of the future is going to be based on energy as well.

NICHOLAS

Absolutely.

ZOLAR

What would you say to other mainline psychiatrists who are struggling with the same kind of issues you did? They see that psychiatry works, but it doesn't work! ...that it takes a long time, and that many people never really get well! What would you say to these persons about RoHun?

NICHOLAS

I would tell them that there are other methods out there that might supply them with what they need. And to search!

Fortunately, in psychiatry, hypnosis ... for instance ... is somewhat mainline. Then there's Milton Erickson, who came out with another whole approach to hypnosis.

I feel they are going to be more amenable, as time goes on.

There are more people, in the field, doing their own kind of work now.

ZOLAR

Do you think as RoHun becomes more popular, perhaps even as a result of this book, people will go to a psychiatrist or psychologist and say, "I've heard about this therapy," just like they did with penicillin and other new drugs?

NICHOLAS

Of course.

ZOLAR

Let me ask you one final question. What personal qualities do you think a RoHun therapist should have?

NICHOLAS

Number one, they should have a desire to grow and heal themselves. A tremendous desire, a real willingness to do it!

Number two, I think they should have capacity for love. They may not know all that love is ... who knows what love is all about ... but they must have that.

Number three, they must have a way with people that allows them to be empathetic, to reach some empathy.

The other thing is they believe that they have healing ability. They don't have to KNOW that they are healers, but they must be willing to acknowledge that we are our OWN healers.

Christ said, "Physician, heal thyself."

They must be willing to believe that that is possible for them. They must be dedicated channels. They must be willing to open up to a whole new area and commit to their growth.

Because as you do RoHun, you grow as well.

It continues in that way.

ZOLAR

That's fantastic. So how are you going to continue to use this, to continue to grow?

NICHOLAS

One of the things I have had to contend with is my fellow psychiatrists and professionals who say, "Well, it's a short-term therapy, and it has a little place, you know. But you are using mesmerism, and a little mumble jumble. You are just being creative and getting..."

Basically, they are just down-playing the reality of what RoHun is all about!

ZOLAR

Why are they doing this? Is it because they are afraid? Because they don't understand it? Do they see it as a threat?

NICHOLAS

I think it is several things. On a larger scale, not just RoHun, but all the alternative therapies are an economic threat.

Since medicine is basically an economic machine, this is one reason.

The other thing is that we, as humans, have a tendency to speak out, and judge something we never have experienced. I have found that many people who talk about alternative therapies have never tried them themselves, until they are desperate, and the system doesn't work.

ZOLAR

So then you see M.D.s sneaking in and out of the backdoors of Chiropractors.

NICHOLAS

Exactly! I went to California recently to learn about a new therapy for physical illness.

The guy who was sitting next to me was an internist, who teaches at a medical school.

Here he has this big, baseball size tumor he shrank to nothing; and has come back for another treatment.

I asked him what he thought of this.

He said, "Miraculous. It works"

I said, 'Would you ever consider using it, or doing it, with your own people?'

He just shook his head, "No."

ZOLAR

Little minds lead little lives, I guess! One of the best stories I heard was about Benjamin Palmer, the founder of chiropractic. One day he was having an argument with an M.D. over chiropractic theory. He left the good doctor shaking his head, and said to his students, "Some minds are like concrete, poured and set!"

NICHOLAS

I like that. Oh, one more thing I wanted to add.

What I have noticed with RoHun is that now we can address in the RoHun process the different levels of the psyche. We can try to understand them and have an opportunity to research them.

The biographical area, of course, deals with our current life experiences. We can get into the prenatal area that deals with birth related trauma, and then, the transpersonal area.

ZOLAR

Are you saying that from RoHun there might emerge a new geography of the psyche, which no one really has?

NICHOLAS

I think so ... and its relationship to the Conscious mind, because we are working with it consciously.

ZOLAR

Do you think that because the RoHun process is so revolutionary and evolutionary right now, it requires the therapist to keep coming back for additional training?

NICHOLAS

Yes. RoHun can be a lifelong process of enlightenment!

CHAPTER EIGHT

TWELVE STEP FOLK AND ROHUN

The terms "spiritual experience" and "spiritual awakening" are used many times in this book which, upon careful reading, shows that the personality change sufficient to bring about recovery from alcoholism has manifested itself among us in many different forms ... Most of us think this awareness of a Power greater than ourselves is the essence of spiritual experience. Our more religious members call it "God-consciousness.

The BIG BOOK, Alcoholics Anonymous

In March 1976, when the Third Edition of Alcoholics Anonymous legendary "BIG BOOK" was published, worldwide membership was estimated at more than one million persons with some 28,000 groups meeting in over 90 countries.

Little did Bill W. and Doctor Bob, co-founders of A.A., imagine the far-reaching implications of their Twelve Step program, which would in time be extended to include both drugs and eating addictions as well.

Recent years see the further extension of so-called Twelve Step programs into a number of psychological areas, including co-dependency.

As it is often touted, no one or no thing can stop a great idea whose time has come, so it is no wonder that the highly spiritual basis of the Twelve Step approach now finds fertile soil in the gardens of this Aquarian Age.

In order that we might best understand exactly how this universally accepted program dovetails with the philosophy of RoHun, following are the Twelve Steps as originally presented in the Big Book:

1- *We admitted we were powerless over alcohol that our lives had become unmanageable.*

2- *Came to believe that a Power greater than ourselves could restore us to sanity.*

3- *Made a decision to turn our will and our lives over to the care of God 'as we understood Him.'*

4- *Made a searching and fearless moral inventory of ourselves.*

5- *Admitted to God, to ourselves, and to another human being the exact nature of our wrongs.*

6- *Were entirely ready to have God remove all these defects of character.*

7- *Humbly asked Him to remove our shortcomings.*

8- *Made a list of all persons we had harmed, and became willing to make amends.*

9- *Made direct amends to such people wherever possible, except when to do so would injure them or others.*

10- *Continued to take personal inventory and when we were wrong promptly admitted it.*

11-Sought through prayer and meditation to improve our conscious contact with God 'as we understood Him,' praying only for knowledge of His will for us and the power to carry that out.

12-Having had a spiritual awakening as the result of these steps, we tried to carry this message to alcoholics, and to practice these principles in all our affairs.

What follows is a most remarkable story of one woman's successful attempt to combine RoHun and The Twelve Steps.

I had the pleasure of meeting and speaking with this woman, who in keeping with the traditions of A.A., we will simply call Ms." C," while visiting Delphi.

Much of what follows is totally her own story, told in her own words, in order to help others whose lives, (unfortunately), may have taken a similar turn...

"I started smoking pot when I was nine years old. I started recovery when I was 24. My drugs of choice were alcohol and cocaine. Towards the end of my using, I strictly used cocaine and alcohol.

"There would be times when I would stay up for ten days in a row with no sleep and no food.

"Cocaine is really painful to come down from, so you want to keep doing more and more, because withdrawals are awful.

"It's not as if you get really sick like heroin but, emotionally, you will go to almost any length to get more! I didn't rob a bank, or do any of that stuff, but at that time

I would try to get 'it' to the best of my ability.
"I tried to quit on my own for two years and I couldn't.
"My dad had gone to work. I got into a really big fight with my boyfriend. I was lying out on the deck crying and drinking Jack Daniels, straight out of the bottle, to come down so I could sleep.
"I was just crying and praying, "God please help me. I can't do it myself. And I don't know where to go."
"Later on that evening, my boyfriend, my dad and myself got together and I told them what was going on.
"They knew what was going on because there were two prior hospitalizations for cocaine and alcohol overdoses.
"So, I told them.
"The next day I ended up in a treatment center, where I was locked up for four months!
"When I got in there and saw the work I had to do, I wanted out. And I would have gotten out, but I couldn't because the door was locked.
"You just have to realize that when you do drugs, your life becomes unmanageable, and the consequences are too high. You have a choice. You can continue to do drugs, and pay the consequences, or you can seek recovery, and start living a better life.
"For a long time it was fun using drugs. I really had some good times. There were many years when it was, and then all of a sudden the consequences were there ... DUI's, throwing up, hangovers, blackouts, seizures, hangovers and overdoses!
"I had crossed a line.
"I had gone from recreational use to abuse and on to full blown addiction!..."

But this is where "Ms. C" came from, where she WAS and not where she IS now!

Today, she tells a decidedly different story...

"I have been involved with RoHun for about five years, and am now a RoHun therapist.

"I started out as a RoHun client.

"When I was younger I was really intuitive like my grandmother. But when I began to use drugs, it was still there, but more on the somewhat dark side.

"When I began to get clean, I began to get clear pictures and feelings about certain events, which would come to fruition. This started scaring me.

"I wanted to learn how to control it and not always be in a psychic frame of mind.

"I wanted to be able to turn it off, and on appropriate times use it for really good things.

"I was sent to a woman to do RoHun. After a couple of sessions with her, she suggested that I should go up to Patricia's, and that's what I did.

"Essentially, I intertwined RoHun with psychotherapy. It was good.

"That way I could go in and do some intense work, and really cry and let out some feelings, because from the RoHun I was so relaxed.

"My therapist was open minded about the RoHun.

"The two worked well together. Sometimes I would go in after RoHun therapy, and process a little bit more, and deal with daily issues and feelings.

"I probably had twenty RoHun sessions..."

At this point in our conversation, I asked "Ms. C" to explain exactly how RoHun helped her more traditional psychotherapy.

"In RoHun, you are so relaxed and your physical eyes are shut, so there is one less sense on some level that you are using. You are laying down and real comfortable.

"I think for me it was easier to let out some of the traumatic issues and really cry, really yell and really get angry.

"I hated to go to psychotherapy, and sit in a chair in an office and cry and scream and yell for two hours. I would be exhausted after this.

"With the RoHun, though, you are so relaxed, it's easier to get more out."

I asked "Ms. C" what kind of traditional therapy her therapist used and what kind of things she was dealing with.

"She used Gestalt Therapy. The things she mainly worked with me on was that when I was growing up, there were three different aspects to myself, almost like a multiple personality. There was a child, an adolescent and an adult.

"We worked on healing my little girl from issues that happened while growing up and integrating her with my adolescent and my adult.

"With this, RoHun helped a lot, because in RoHun you deal with the ten year old, and you can get a clear picture of what went on around you in your environment with the process.

"Integrating this with psychotherapy was really wonderful."

At this point I asked for more details as to how "Ms. C" came to RoHun to begin with:

"It was God's will that I hooked up with RoHun.

"I had a sponsor in the Program. I felt I was going crazy, insane and didn't tell anybody for a long time about my thoughts.

"So, finally I told my best friend.

"She said, 'You need to tell your sponsor.'

"I finally got up enough nerve to tell her. She said I should go see this lady.

"I made an appointment to do RoHun with her, and found out that lots of people see and hear things before they happen!

"It's not abnormal. It's perfectly OK. You are not crazy.

"To find out that there was nothing wrong with me was wonderful..."

I asked "Ms. C" if she would recommend RoHun to everyone who is in psychotherapy. She replied: "For me, RoHun has been faster. It does zero in on specific situations that are going on with me. I think that psychotherapy is good, too.

"It would depend on the person and where they are with themselves.

"There have been times when RoHun was not appropriate, because I needed to sit down and go slowly. "I think my issues were very deep. It was important to be able to take a little longer time, on a weekly basis to process..."

At this point, "Ms. C" is happily employed as a spiritual counselor at a psychiatric hospital and is currently studying for her B.A. in Psychology. I asked her where she saw herself going with her unique combination of psychotherapy, RoHun and Twelve Step work!

"I see myself working with a lot of recovering people as well as continuing my college education.

"RoHun is very aligned with Twelve Step work because in the program the Fourth Step requires a fearless and searching moral inventory, which you have to admit to another being.

"This is almost identical to what happens in the RoHun therapy process. "The principles behind the program ... honesty, integrity, brotherly love, faith, courage ... are all found in RoHun.

"Also in both RoHun and Twelve Step work, it's a 'God of your understanding,' and not a god that someone makes for you in a church, although it could be.

"It is whatever you are most comfortable with in your heart.

"The lady who did RoHun on me, initially, was also in recovery, so it made a lot of sense to me.

"Yes, they are very much alike.

"If anyone wants to deeply change, they can break any negative, or so-called, bad patterns, they want. I think RoHun really helps that, because you are able to get so deep into your gut and your soul about it that it's easier.

"My going through RoHun helps me to be a better spiritual counselor..."

What do others think of "Ms. C" and the work she has done?

"A lot of people admire my program. I have such a high level of acceptance and serenity that other people want it!

"They want to know 'how' I got it.

"Part of the program is sharing, so if they want to come to me, or another RoHun therapist, that's fine.

"I feel really confident that whatever the God of my understanding's will is for me happens. If I am to have clients, they will be drawn to me.

"Or if I am supposed to do traditional therapy, that's the path that will unfold. Whatever unfolds, that's fine!"

And what has RoHun done, and continues to do, for "Ms. C?"

"I think with me it has given a new freedom inside my soul.

"It has made me a better counselor, a better person.

"And not only this ... I am happy, real happy!

"It's from within, not from a new coat or car. It's deep from within and it never goes away.

"Unlike drugs, I don't ever have to come down. And I don't ever go through withdrawals.

"Also, I am learning what real love is. It's so beautiful. There are no words for it.

"If you are on your own, RoHun is a powerful technique to discover what real love is.

"It has made my life very beautiful, worthy and so many things.

"I guess I could go on forever about the positive aspects.

"Now, my life is full of love, and passion, and gratitude.

"If someone is walking around feeling 'that' 28 days a month, that's really incredible!"

Perhaps you, the reader, know someone like "Ms. C." who is also in a Twelve Step program.

If so, tell him or her about RoHun.

Sharing could make a big difference for them, too!

CHAPTER NINE

REINCARNATION AND ROHUN

Rebirth, not of a changeless soul, but of an ever-evolving, karma-created bundle of characteristics is accepted by the whole world east of Karachi, and only in the West must text-books of Buddhism give it space. The evolving consciousness achieves successive states of spiritual achievement until the last, to our mortal knowledge, is reached in Buddhahood. Only then is the self entirely dead, to rise no more, and the Self, released from the last of its Fetters, is merged as a dewdrop in the Shining Sea.
Christmas Humphreys, BUDDHISM

When Christmas Humphreys, the renown Buddhist scholar, wrote the words above in 1949, only a small portion of the Western world seemed ready to accept the idea of "reincarnation" and "previous lives."

While these old ideas were too often touted in Theosophical circles, the general public cared little about such things, referring to those who did as "strange" or "weird."

For me, personally, I can't recall when I first came into contact with the idea of having lived before. It might have been when I first began to study Yoga at the age of twelve.

Having been very psychic as a child, I recall an early dream about Indians. The next day, while playing in the yard, I unearthed an old arrowhead. But this could have been "clairvoyance," and not that I was tuning in to another lifetime.

When I became older, I recall my puzzlement at the fact that the idea of reincarnation, which made so much sense, was not a part and parcels of Christianity. This bothered me greatly, and was one of the reasons I later abandoned my Methodist roots in favor of New Thought.

Later on, when I began to teach various courses in metaphysics at the famed New School for Social Research in New York City, one of the courses I delighted in teaching was entitled simply, "Recalling Previous Lives."

By then, however, I had gotten it somewhat together, both academically and personally, as to what I really believed about the subject.

I remember going to hear various speakers, often quite aged, at the Theosophical Society talk "about" reincarnation. I must say, however, that their lectures were usually quite dry and boring, somewhat like eating shredded wheat without milk!

It was not until I began a course in Jungian analysis, under the guidance of the late Erlo Van Waveren, himself a direct disciple of Jung (although the word "disciple" would probably bother him), did I come to terms with the 'experiential' side of reincarnation.

For me, this came in the form of information that was brought through by a well known medium and spiritualist, Ethel Myers; information that I was eventually able to research and validate.

I was told WHO I had been ... WHAT I had done and ... WHERE I had lived.

I was given MY NAME in that other lifetime and told exactly HOW I had died.

However, the fact that this person had existed in no way proved to my satisfaction that I WAS that person!

One could simply be tuning in to Jung's Collective Unconscious, someplace, somewhere, somehow.

It was only later on, as a result of Jungian analysis, that I began to have dreams of having lived before, dreams that would forever alter the future course of my life.

But it is not my intention, dear reader, to sell you on the idea that reincarnation is a reality. Much like gravity, you will have to find this out for yourself!

Rather, it is my intent to simply share with you the "possibility" that such may be true, since one cannot totally comprehend the RoHun process without this philosophic understanding.

I seem to recall as a child learning the maxim in physics that, "Energy can neither be created nor destroyed."

Assuming this is so, it is only a small step to the realization that since the RoHun process is energy based, the energy it works with must have always been, is now, and always will be!

In other words, this is the "Force" that Luke Skywalker came to realize.

This is the very same ONENESS the Great Master spoke of when he said, "Before Abraham was, I Am."

We are getting ahead of ourselves...

To begin with, reincarnation, though controversial, has been accepted by Hindus and Buddhists since the dawn of their faiths.

Simply put, such a doctrine implies that we are "embodied anew" from lifetime to lifetime, in the same manner one might adorn a new suit or set of clothes.

In other words, after an undetermined period of existence in the OTHER world or dimension, the soul of a deceased person attaches itself to a new human parent, and is REBORN in THIS world, in accordance with its failures or accomplishments in the life previous!

As what is being reborn is the SOUL ... a fragment of the divine ... ultimately such will return to the Godhead, its divine source.

In order for this to happen, however, the soul must pass through all of life's experiences, which is far too much to be comprehended by a single sojourn on the Earth plane.

Also, as the experiences of being MALE are decidedly different from inhabiting a FEMALE body, it is likely that each soul will inhabit bodies of each of the sexes along its journey.

Eventually, through successive rebirths, this soul will reach a state of Cosmic Consciousness, after which the necessity of being reborn, unless by choice, will no longer exist.

The poet Holland best describes the journey in this way:

Heaven is not reached by a single bound;
But we climb the ladder by which we rise,
From the lowly earth to the vaulted skies,
And we mount to its summit round by round.

In a somewhat lighter fashion, England's Poet Laureate, Rudyard Kipling, long influenced by Indian philosophy, adds:

We do come back, — come back again,
— As long as this big earth rolls.
He Who never wasted a leaf of a tree,
Do you think he could squander souls?

Besides Hindus and Buddhists, various Roman writers held that the belief in reincarnation, in some form, was found among the Druids and Gauls.

Likewise, in Greece, the schools of Orpheus and Pythagoras also ascribed to its doctrine.

In the conclusion of the famed "Republic," Plato also mentions the doctrine.

Many scholars also attest to the acceptance of this belief among the Essenes, of which Jesus was likely a member, the Pharisees, Karaites, and other Jewish and semi-Jewish religious groups.

Later on, both the Neoplatonists and Gnostics were also found to embrace a similar view.

When it comes to Christianity, the philosophic waters of the early church fathers were muddied indeed.

For St. Jerome (340-420) it was his belief that reincarnation had been taught and accepted by the early Christians as a 'secret doctrine' communicated to a select group of the Master's disciples.

Origen (186-253) believed that only a belief in reincarnation could explain certain scriptural passages, which the early church fathers had somehow forgotten to delete, when they arbitrarily decided what "would" and "would not" be included in the Bible.

Clearly, when the Master Jesus asked his disciples, "Whom do men say that I the Son of man, am?" and they replied, "Some say that thou art John the Baptist: some, Elias; and others, Jeremias, or one of the prophets," both he and they were referring to the belief in reincarnation! (Matthew 16:14)

Later on in this same gospel, Jesus makes it clear that it is not he who "is/was" Elias, but rather John the Baptist.

"But I say unto you, That Elias has come already, and they knew him not, but have done unto him whatsoever they listed. Likewise shall also the Son of man suffer of them." (Matthew 17:12)

In yet another passage, the disciples ask Jesus to explain how it is that a man is born blind, "Master, who did sin, this man, or his parents, that he was born blind?" (John 9:2)

Certainly if one is BORN blind at birth, he had no time to sin in "this lifetime." Either his parents sinned, and he carries their sin, or the sinning took place BEFORE this lifetime!

To this Jesus replied, "Neither hath this man sinned, nor his parents, but that the works of God should be made manifest in him."

In still another passage, Jesus says, "Except a man be born again, he cannot see the kingdom of God." (John 3)

In reply Nicodemus, apparently not comprehending Jesus' meaning says, "How can a man be born when he is old? Can he enter the second time into his mother's womb, and be born?"

Jesus' answer is clear, "Verily, verily I say unto thee, Except a man be born of water and of the Spirit, he cannot enter into the Kingdom of God. That which is born of the flesh is flesh; and that which is born of the Spirit is spirit."

In other words, it is not the man of flesh that Jesus is speaking of, but rather the soul which attains Cosmic Consciousness (i.e., born of water.)

Out of frustration that Nicodemus still does not grasp his meaning, Jesus asks, "Art thou a master of Israel, and knowest not these things?"

In fact, so hot was the issue surrounding this belief in reincarnation, the Emperor Justinian (553) convened the Second Council of Constantinople which issued the edict, "If anyone assert the fabulous pre-existence of souls, and shall submit to the monstrous doctrine that follows from it, let him be anathema."

While for many Christians the belief in reincarnation is itself predetermined by the particular faith to which they ascribe, modern exponents who are not Hindus or Buddhists include Theosophists, Anthroposophists and certain Spiritualists.

In the case of the first two, many of their ideas have in fact been drawn from Hindu and Buddhist sources.

When it comes to the Spiritualists, those interested are best referred to my book, ZOLAR's "BOOK OF THE SPIRITS," in which I discuss in great length the various spiritualist arguments both "for" and "against" the subject.

Generally speaking, it may be said that traditional (orthodox) spiritualism does not believe in reincarnation, preferring instead the idea that to be reborn would be to "go backwards," rather than ever evolve towards the Godhead.

A dominant exception to this is found in the teachings of "spiritist" Allan Kardec who writes:

The doctrine of our freedom in the choice of our successive existences and of the trials which we have to undergo ceases to appear strange when we consider that spirits, being freed from matter, judge of things differently from men. They perceive the ends which these trials are intended to work out ends far more important to them than the fugitive enjoyments of earth. After each existence they see the steps they have already accomplished, and comprehend what they still lack for the attainment of that purity which alone will enable them to reach the goal; and they willingly submit to the vicissitudes of corporeal life, demanding of their own accord to be allowed to undergo those which will aid them to advance most rapidly. There is, therefore, nothing surprising in a spirit making choice of a hard or painful life. He knows that in his state of imperfection he cannot enjoy the perfect happiness to which he aspires; but he obtains a glimpse of that happiness, and seeks to effect his own improvement, as the sole means of its attainment.

Clarification must also be made of the different viewpoints as to the form in which the soul returns to the earth plane.

Certain Hindu sects hold that the soul may regress and be reborn as a plant or an animal. For instance, the early

Hindu law-giver Manu held that anyone who killed a Brahmin would enter the womb of a sow or she-ass! Likewise, a drunkard may be reborn as a bird who lives on dung!

On the other hand most Western schools of belief hold that once the human form has been reached in its evolution, one can never revert to the animal kingdom.

This does not prevent one from "acting like an ass," only being born as one!

Still other critics would argue, "If reincarnation is a fact, why is it that we do not recall our previous lives?"

In Plato's "Republic," an answer is offered in the idea that each soul, before incarnating, drinks from a river in the Plain of Forgetfulness, so that his choice of the next life is not hampered by what happened in the past.

Exactly WHY one person recalls a previous life, and another does not, is not yet known. Certainly the idea that we have forgotten a previous life does not in any way logically preclude it from having taken place.

For instance, most of us spend about one third of our lives "sleeping," recalling little of what happened in this state.

A most extraordinary exposition of previous lives in action is found in the recently published work, "MANY LIVES, MANY MASTERS," written by Brian L. Weiss, MD.

Dr. Weiss, a graduate of Columbia University and Yale Medical School, is currently Chairman of Psychiatry at the Mount Sinai Medical Center in Miami.

When one of his patients began to recall past-life traumas which were the origin of her recurring nightmares and anxiety attacks, this traditional psychotherapist began to challenge his own linear thinking.

Going on to cure this patient, and others, by using past-life therapy, he began to embark on what could very well have been the end of his previously successful career. Of this he writes:

It took me four years to write about what happened, four years to garner the courage to take the professional risk of revealing this unorthodox information... In the wee hours of the morning, I thought of my old Hungarian grandfather who had died while I was still a teenager. Whenever I would tell him I was afraid to take a risk, he would lovingly encourage me by repeating his favorite English expression: "Vat the hell, "he would say, "vat the hell."

In yet another attempt to answer, "Why do we not remember?," Christmas Humphreys suggests the following:

It is often asked why we do not remember our past lives. The answer is clear. Because physical memory needs a physical brain, and the brain which remembers incidents of this life is different from that which registered the deeds of the one before. But in fact the bridge from life to life is often crossed. Students claim to have trained their memories to go back step by step until they arrive at an accurate memory of their previous life or lives. The subsequent verification of remembered

*scenery, surroundings and events, seems
to prove the truth of the experimenter's
claims, and the Buddhist scriptures show
examples of this interesting but unprofit-
able exercise.*
BUDDHISM, p. 106

In the philosophy of Carl G. Jung are found very definite
ideas concerning the various forms of rebirth which, in their
definition, embrace the necessity for recollection of earlier
lifetimes:

*This concept of rebirth necessarily implies
the continuity of personality. Here the
human personality is regarded as continuous and accessible to memory, so
that, when one is incarnated or born, one
is able, at least potentially, to remember
that one has lived through previous existences and that these existences were one's
own, i.e., that they had the same ego-form
as the present life. As a rule, reincarnation
means rebirth in a human body.*
COLLECTED WORKS, 9.1, 201

In yet another place in these writings, Jung makes it
clear that "hints of previous lives" are ever present in both
the anima and animus, though finding different expression
in each:

*Intimations of reincarnation in the form of
irrational feelings hang very strongly about
a man's anima, while a woman will some-*

*times consciously admit such feelings if
she is not too much under the domination
of the man's rationalism.*
COLLECTED WORKS, 10.87

Although it is not generally known outside of Jung's
magic circle of students, the idea of reincarnation was one
which he held on a personal, experiential level, believing
himself the reincarnation of Paracelsus (1491-1541), the
German-Swiss alchemist and physician; and Goethe (1749-
1832), the German author. Jung, himself, was born in
1875.

In his classic, "MEMORIES, DREAMS, REFLECTIONS,"
first published in 1961, Jung writes:

*I could well imagine that I might have
lived in former centuries and there encountered questions I was not yet able to
answer; that I had to be born again because I had not fulfilled the task that was
given to me. When I die, my deeds will
follow along with me-this is how I imagine
it. I will bring with me what I have done.
In the meantime it is important to insure
that I do not stand at the end with empty
hands. Buddha, too, seems to have had
this thought when he tried to keep his
disciples from wasting time on useless
speculation.*
p. 318

In order to bring our current discussion back into the
context of RoHun, we must simply recall that it was Dr.

RoHun himself whom first presented Patricia with the idea that faulty thought patterns and memories are actually "stored" within the various chakras.

Through experimentation, RoHun therapists discovered that many times, coincidentally, the source of the faulty thought pattern was not in THIS but rather a PREVIOUS lifetime! And it was THIS memory that needed liberation.

In fact, in some instances it has been found that a single faulty thought pattern may actually persist, and repeat itself, from lifetime to lifetime!

Confirming this belief, Shaffica Karagulla, M.D. and Dora van Gelder Kunz write concerning the causal body:

> *According to the doctrine of reincarnation, those fruits of experience which we have transformed into enduring qualities mark the growth or evolution of the individual soul. These are retained from life to life with the causal body which becomes a composite of the highest qualities of the Self ... it is also termed 'causal' because it gathers together the fruits of our long struggles and sacrifices to grow in understanding, and in these lie the true causes of what we are here and now-the seeds of our qualities of mind and heart.*
> THE CHAKRAS, p. 66

If indeed this is so, the only way in which to realign and redirect those energy patterns which in a manner of speaking have gotten stuck somewhere in time is through the RoHun therapy process.

Of this need, the Rosicrucian Joseph J. Weed writes:

*The ensuing lifetime presents the opportu-
nity of paying the debts incurred in
previous lives and of permitting others to
repay you for your help to them. These
debts must be repaid and the energy puri-
fied at the level at which the original
misapplication occurred.*

In other words, what is being said here is a "particular chakra" and a "particular lifetime!"

Continuing with this idea, Christmas Humphreys affirms:

*All action has its due result. A stone thrown
into a pond causes wavelets to circle out-
wards to a distance proportionate to the
initial disturbance; after which the initial
state of equilibrium is restored. And since
each disturbance must start from some
particular point, it is clear that harmony
can be restored only by the reconverging
to that point of the forces set in motion.
Thus the consequences of an act re-act, via
all the universe, upon the doer with a force
commensurate with his own.*

BUDDHISM, p. 103

One might rightly ask, "Given these understandings, could there be RoHun 'without' reincarnation and previous lives?"

Yes, but such would be much like owning a luxury automobile without having gas with which to run it!

In the next chapter we will examine the Individuation process.

You can read this one tomorrow ... if you wish!

CHAPTER TEN

THE LORD OF THE UNDERWORLD

Individuation means becoming a single, homogenous being, and, in so far as "individuality" embraces our innermost, last, and incomparable uniqueness, it also implies becoming one's own self. We could therefore translate individuation as "coming to self-hood" or "self-realization."
Carl G. Jung, TWO ESSAYS, par. 266

By now it should be clear to you, dear reader, that RoHun as we have portrayed it is a VERY special process which, while it has a definite technique and philosophy, can be easily integrated with other therapeutic practices.

The reason for its great flexibility is that it is based on various esoteric principles which accept the fact that in essence we are all dynamic, ever evolving, energy beings.

In other words, although we may be psychologically stuck in the energy of a particular problem, which is contained within a particular chakra, we always possess the ability to go in and change that energy in the same manner one dispels darkness by simply turning on the light!

The uniqueness, then, of the RoHun approach is its ability to first discover exactly <u>what</u> and <u>where</u> the problem is, and then to correct it by altering its energy accompaniment.

In a symbolic way, by doing this, one is clearing up all the dark spots in their Soul nature by turning on the lights, one by one, eventually reaching that point spoken of by the Master, "Where the eye is single and the body is full of light." Certainly another word for this process is "individuation," and it is here, once again, that RoHun finds credence for its beliefs, this time in the teachings of Carl G. Jung.

To comprehend exactly what Jung means by individuation, we must place it within the context of his entire philosophy, and especially the "persona" with which it clearly stands in opposition.

For Jung the construction of the persona, or mask, means a formidable concession to all that the external world stands for. In other words, a self-sacrifice to the point at which people actually believe what they are pretending to be.

When it comes to individuation, Jung's requirement is that:

> Strict differentiation from the collective psyche is absolutely necessary, since partial or blurred differentiation leads to an immediate melting away of the individual in the collective.

In other words, Jung is saying one must break away, and as Thoreau suggested, "March to the sounds of a different drummer," if one is to exchange the <u>persona</u> for the self-realized.

In so doing, however, one is actually becoming more complete in terms of the collective qualities of the human being since the peculiarity is no longer being suppressed.

One way in which Jung expresses individuation is this:

I use the term "individuation" to denote
the process by which a person becomes a
psychological "individual," that is, a sepa-
rate, indivisible unity or "whole."
Collected Works, Vol. 9i, 490

In other words, just as a drop of water taken from the ocean both IS and IS NOT the ocean from which it has been taken, so does a person find himself after the Grail Quest has begun.

Under no circumstances can individua-
tion be the unique goal of psychological
education. Before individuation can be
taken for a goal, the educational aim of
adaptation to the necessary minimum of
collective standards must first be attained.
Psychological Types, p. 562

Certainly, the RoHun maxim, "We are many, we are One," addresses this very same idea.

Through the RoHun process, one begins to perceive the unconscious self as both cause and effect of that which he or she is; which in time, leads one to "consciousness," which Jung calls, "the supreme arbiter."

According to Jung, the solution to the individuation puzzle is both simple and complex; paradoxical, much like the Zen <u>koans</u>. "The answer lies in getting rid of the separation between the conscious and the unconscious," Jung suggests, which in a way is exactly what RoHun does through its unique technique.

Yet another word for individuation is "undividedness,"

which for Jung means not separating one from his instincts, and his or her source, the unconscious.

In his almost heretical work, "Answer To Job," Jung writes:

> *The more consciousness a man possesses the more he is separated from his instincts (which at least give him an inkling of the hidden wisdom of God) and the more prone he is to error.*

Putting it another way, what is needed, then, is a way in which one can achieve contact with the unconscious. For Jung, one way in which to do this, which is universally accepted, is meditation.

For RoHun clients and practitioners, this is easily accomplished, oftentimes during the three basic RoHun sessions.

Colin Wilson in his biography of Jung, "Lord Of The Underworld," seeks to explain this point as follows:

> *Let us look more closely at this concept of individuation. Why does Jung regard it as a passive process? Because he sees it as a flow from the unconscious to the conscious. It has to be that way around because the conscious, has, so to speak, no way of clambering down a ladder into the unconscious ... The therapist is, so to speak, the midwife to the unconscious.*

p. 139

While Wilson was correct in his understanding that there was no way for the unconscious to be reached through the conscious, except through a technique like meditation, such is no longer true.

Through the discovery of the RoHun process, and in its unique, simultaneous linking of the unconscious and conscious minds of both the client and therapist, one gains the ability to do just this ... climb down the ladder to the unconscious!

Wolfgang Hochheimer in his work, "The Psychotherapy of C. G. Jung," concludes his discussion with the following further definition of individuation by Jung as, "an integration or <u>completeness</u> of the individual, who in this way approaches <u>wholeness</u> but not <u>perfection</u>, which is the ideal of certain world philosophies."

It is here that RoHun practitioners find themselves in total agreement with Jung's ideology, but able to offer a unique process by which integration is accomplished.

One can only wonder at what Jung would say, after experiencing or witnessing an actual RoHun session.

According to Colin Wilson:

> *For Jung, personally, individuation meant the ability to surrender himself to the 'subjective mind' as in the waking fantasies he called 'active imagination.'*
> Ibid, p. 88

It is interesting to note Wilson's emphasis here on Jung's use of what he called "active imagination," for it is this very process that is utilized in a very special way by RoHun practitioners to guide their clients into the depths of their innermost being.

Lastly, mention must be made of that part of the RoHun session in which the therapist and client actually contact various fragments of the psyche which seemingly occupy the different chakras.

Jung's comments on such an unusual practice are, once again, surprisingly supportive:

> *Every form of communication with the split-off part of the psyche is therapeutically effective.*
> Alchemical Studies, p. 463

What better way to end this chapter on RoHun and Jung than by recalling these words from our "Lord of the Underworld,"

> *Individuation does not shut one out from the world, but gathers the world to oneself.*

To this RoHun practitioners can only say," Amen!"

CHAPTER ELEVEN

CORPORATE BOARD ROOMS
AND ROHUN

Finally, brethren, whatsoever things are
true, whatsoever things are honest, what-
soever things are just, whatsoever things
are pure, whatsoever things are lovely,
whatsoever things are of good report; if
there be any virtue, and if there be any
praise, think on these things.
PHILIPPIANS 4:8

By now you have seen that RoHun practitioners come from all walks of life. One might say that they are essentially "chosen" to do this work and actually have little choice when it comes to refusing to follow their inner calling.

While at Delphi I had the opportunity to talk with two very special RoHun devotees whose backgrounds come from what might be called the "corporate scene."

The first, Marshall Smith, is a director of The RoHun Institute and the Extension of Life Foundation, and is Patricia Hayes' husband. I first met Marshall while writing THE BOOK OF THE SPIRITS. At the time of our first meeting, Marshall was employed as a vice president with the Kimberly Clark Corporation.

The second, Joyce Rennolds, whose calling card reads, "Motivator of One or a Thousand," has presented seminars through out the United States for many of the Fortune 500 corporations.

Together, Joyce and Marshall represent what I would like to think of as a new breed of cat. Namely, persons in the corporate, materialistic world who have taken the time to discover and actually use their spirituality.

Recently, Marshall Smith chose to elect an early retirement in order that he and Patricia might pursue the fulfillment of the RoHun work "full time."

While one often thinks of retirement as that time of life when one begins to take things easy, such is certainly not the case for Marshall, as he openly confessed to me that his corporate activities were duck soup compared to the demands placed upon him by the RoHun activities.

Although he spent many, many years directing corporate activities, his early spiritual experiences somewhat predicted the place he now occupies.

"It might be of interest to you, too, that as a child and a young person I was raised in a Fundamentalist family ... Pentecostal ... The Assembly of God," Marshall was quick to share.

"I recall going to Oral Roberts' tents when he was on the road. I saw physical healings that could not be explained in any other way except they were miracles. This sparked my inquisitive mind and launched me into a lifelong study of the spiritual world."

Marshall's personal feelings about RoHun were summed up by him in one word, "Phenomenal!"

"It's more than something you find in some building in some remote place like Delphi. It's a way of life that Patricia and I live. Continually we use RoHun and work with the chakras. When we recognize some action or reaction that does not harmonize with our normal patterns, we use RoHun to find the source of this response. RoHun has been a significant means of our growth."

I asked Marshall if, in his opinion, RoHun was something that couples should do together.

He answered, "Yes. I look at it like this. In my religious training there is a word I dislike, because of its obvious misuse. Unfortunately, I don't know of one to replace it with. The word is 'Soul.' The church has struggled with this word from its beginning. RoHun provides a means around this dilemma."

Marshall continued, "If you seek out a religious person and ask, 'What is the Soul?' One can't get a definite answer! It's something up there, in here, out there, that somehow makes a decision where it goes at the death of the body. What RoHun does is it gives dimension to the Soul ... what it is, where it is and how to work with it to make it grow. With these dimensions it begins to take on the aura of science in the spiritual area. I think this is phenomenal."

While Marshall was busy working his way to the top of the corporate ladder, he also pastored a church, trying to feed the spiritual side of himself.

When it comes to the connection between RoHun and business, Marshall's comments are more than just interesting.

"It's hard to really describe it specifically, but in business you must keep an emotional, mental, and feeling balance which is really how your body energies work. When you approach situations, you approach them differently. You don't just take a hard approach, and go full speed ahead. You feel the various energy centers integrate with each other, and you know where you are. You don't get so up tight!"

Marshall added, "You flow with the situation in a multifaceted approach, rather, than just mentally push it along, disregarding peripheral events and feelings of others."

I asked Marshall if, as a corporate executive, his stress could also come from other sources than just the job ... for instance, the home and family as well?

"Of course, the demand for your time in the corporate environment is tremendous. At times it seems as if your job is your whole life. Providing adequate time for your family, considering the job requirements, often times brings significant stress. Until I acquired tools such as RoHun, I felt my performance in this area of life was poor."

Can the RoHun process actually increase one's on-the-job creativity?

"Definitely. When I started with RoHun I observed a big change! The freedom to create became a continually evolving process rather than, 'Hey, I have to think up something quick!' You begin to understand that the flow of ideas will continue to come as long as you remain relaxed in the situation."

Marshall continued to think out loud.

"The effect on me has been profound. My decision to step out (i.e. elect early retirement). I could have stayed in the corporate life for another six years making super money. But I looked at it and said, 'Hey, I am sitting here giving my life away. I can't accept that!"

Did RoHun increase Marshall's personal efficiency?

"Very much so. I could do tremendous amounts of work in short periods of time where, it used to just drive me down into the ground!"

Marshall continued.

"Without the knowledge that has come out of RoHun and the peacefulness it brings, I don't think I would have had the confidence to step out of my corporate job. Patricia and I determined that RoHun is our life and our mission, whatever comes of it.

"I accept that. This is what we have both dedicated the rest of our lives to, and we are happy about it."

At this point, I could not keep Marshall's enthusiasm from bursting out.

"One of the things that RoHun does is to cause you to observe reactions you have, like in business. You recognize it and say, 'Hey, that's a different reaction. Why am I reacting that way?' So you immediately say, 'I have to go and find out what it was.' You become sensitive to those kind of reactions. You ask the question about the reaction rather than the situation. I am then concerned with my inner self as much as with the outside event. So I would go home and say, 'Patricia, I acted this way. Let's go in and find out why.'

"To me this is phenomenal. You begin to consider your own inner health. To my way of thinking, RoHun is a natural continuation of the old Pythagorean saying, 'KNOW THYSELF.' It is a means and a method by which we can look inside and get results."

Surely Marshall's words about getting results clearly toll the corporate bells, for getting results by any means has long been accepted as the way of the materialistic warrior!

Perhaps a better ending to our brief conversation could never be found than in his final comments.

"To me, RoHun gets into that area that the Apostle

James in the Bible talks about when he tells us to 'think on these things.' RoHun gets into this very area and works on your thoughts, teaching you to think. We can say that the physical dimension IS the thought dimension. During the time between your thought and execution of it, you have time to correct it, IF YOU WANT TO."

Thank you Marshall. We will talk to you again later on....

......

Joyce Rennolds was born in Lansing, Michigan and was raised in Detroit.

Already alluded to, her biographical sketch reads like a Triple A tour through "Who's Who in the Corporate World."

Currently residing in Atlanta, a few of her best known clients include Georgia State University, Kent State University, Scott Paper Company, New York Life Insurance, Delta Air Lines, American Management Society, Atlanta Business Network, Mary Kay Cosmetics, John Portman Company, US Department of Interior, Small Business Administration, Lions Club, Rotary Club, Chamber of Commerce, World Trade Council, etc.

In addition, she has spoken at and conducted seminars for various churches of all denominations, numerous government agencies and countless alcohol and substance abuse programs.

Clearly, she has earned the title, "Motivator of One or a Thousand!" and remains a classic role model for the truly professional woman in business.

Surely, if you want to throw a parade or set off a firecracker that rocks the neighborhood, there's no one better than Joyce to make it happen!

But, like Marshall Smith, there's another side to Joyce that not everyone is privy to, but which she willingly shared with us.

"I am a professional speaker and a motivator. This is my tag. Motivator of One or a Thousand," she says.

She was led to meet Patrica Hayes by a man named Bob Proctor who insisted that she go and hear her speak.

Of this, Joyce comments, "I went to hear her and was absolutely amazed at how she could tune in to somebody and read them. I said. 'I want to do that.' I had a similar gift when I was growing up. My family was very, very strict Catholic so I was supposed to put things like spirits away. When I did, however, I also lost the idea of creating things with my mind.

"I went to parochial school, eventually left the church, and as a matter of fact, was later excommunicated.

"After leaving Catholicism, I studied Norman Vincent Peale, Ben Sweetland, Ernest Holmes, Manly Palmer Hall and even Claire Prophet.

"What I found was that I could glean the truth from these books and pull out information that fit and resonated for me at the core level. So I started to take this into the market place, which is what I do today.

"Still another person that was influential in my life was Earl Nightingale. I spent five years with the Nightingale-Conant corporation first selling their programs, and then lecturing for them.

"It was at this time that I crashed into severe alcoholism. I was married at the time and was continually traveling on the road, trying to find the one thing that would give me the spiritual essence I was looking for.

"This was thirteen years ago. I stopped drinking.

"I went from mental law into the spiritual realm and found there was a very fine line that took me up there to those higher vibrations.

"Sure, I was speaking, motivating, teaching all of those things ... and talking about laws and principles.

"When Patricia came, it was the final touch that said, 'Here is where it is really at!'

"So getting into Patricia's work, and learning to tune in to people was the start.

"I was in Patricia's second RoHun graduating class in 1983.

"Over the years, I have conducted an average of ten RoHun sessions per month, even though I speak and travel around."

Since Joyce had studied many things before discovering RoHun, I asked her to evaluate its importance. Her answer was more than surprising.

"I suppose if I had to say what the one thing was that influenced me the most as a professional speaker who could go to the top of any corporation, it's the RoHun! It gave me the confidence to know where people are coming from."

Joyce continued. "I have done as many as four RoHun sessions a day, which I don't do now. I have never done any advertising. Not once. I let it come to me. I put it out there and I agree to serve, and do what I have to do to create that. I do a lot of affirmations and visualizations."

As Joyce had been personally involved with the Twelve Step program, and continues to present various seminars for these groups, I asked her to comment on what she thought was its connection with RoHun.

"The Twelve Step program is a beautiful, spiritually based philosophy. A lot of my clients today are in these programs and are going through the Fourth, Fifth and Sixth steps when they are going through RoHun. Many of these clients tell other prospective clients, 'When you go to Joyce and go through RoHun, you can't lie, because the image that's true always comes up! This is because RoHun works with guilt, shame and denial."

Returning to the connection between RoHun and the corporation, I asked Joyce what she felt RoHun could do for the corporate executive under stress. Like Marshall, her answer was quite extraordinary!

"It can absolutely set them free. It really can because this is what it does. When men come to me from the corporate environment, they usually come in and they are very, very businesslike. I do not alter the RoHun process, but I do play down the fact that it is channeled."

As for the changing roles of the sexes seen in today's business world, Joyce shared the following.

"Men are getting in touch with the feminine energy they never had before. Men will now sit there and cry, and feel, and experience. I am now writing a new book, and want to say in it that many women do not understand the sensitivity of the male. They think that a male is totally unfeeling! That really is not true. It is a lie because there are a lot of men who are totally feeling and can't express it, because they are closed at the heart."

Since Joyce has also addressed a number of groups centering around codependency, I asked her to comment on this as well.

"People are becoming aware that they are codependent and that they are not free when they are caught up in that other person. They get caught up in the enmeshment and into all the things that that creates. What I see taking place on planet Earth is a revolution. It is now very, very chic to be in Twelve Step programs!"

Should persons in Twelve Step programs be told about RoHun?

"They have to know that. If I was without RoHun and these other tools, I would be lost. What RoHun does is that it changes the thought patterns," Joyce was quick to respond.

So there you have it...

Two comments from two corporate superstars who have been there.

Just as it is now OK for a "real" man to cry, so can the mainstream corporate executive increase his efficiency and potential for success by adding the RoHun process to his bag of tricks.

Why not?

Marshall Smith and Joyce Rennolds did it!

CHAPTER TWELVE

IS ROHUN JUST ANOTHER CARD GAME?

You may perhaps know of the amusing fact that originally divination was always practiced in the churches. The old Jews, for instance, had a divination oracle in their sanctuaries in Jerusalem and on certain occasions when the priest wanted to consult Jahweh he tried through such oracles to discover the will of God.
MARIE-LOUISE VON FRANZ

Synchronicity takes the coincidence of events in space and time as meaning something more than mere chance, namely, a peculiar interdependence of objective events among themselves as well as with the subjective (psychic) states of the observer or observers.
CARL G. JUNG

By now, dear reader, it must be apparent that while the very practice of RoHun requires experiential training which can only be obtained from the Institute itself, the philosophical ideas behind RoHun are themselves both universal and simple.

Recently a major breakthrough occurred as to how the teaching of RoHun could expand beyond the actual therapeutic process. This breakthrough was channeled through Patricia Hayes and Marshall Smith by Dr. RoHun himself.

Dr. RoHun began the channelling session with these words:
     "RoHun is a transformational system of spiritual psy-
chology, but it is also much more. RoHun is a carrier of four
major thoughts that are vital for man's understanding in the
Age.
     "These four major thoughts, two transformational truths
from Western Philosophy and two transformational truths
from Eastern Philosophy, are the four cornerstones of
RoHun.

WESTERN PHILOSOPHY   1. LOVE
                       2. FORGIVENESS
EASTERN PHILOSOPHY   1. CONTINUATION OF
                          CONSCIOUSNESS-
                          REBIRTH
                       2. SELF KNOWLEDGE

     "Love and forgiveness have been preached for two
thousand years in the West, and man has still not lifted his
energy to the Heart Chakra where Unconditional Love,
Brotherhood and Forgiveness lie waiting to be realized and
expressed.
     "RoHun is a carrier of these four vital transformational
truths. RoHun carries them from the 'outer' world where
they have been taught, to the 'inner' world where they can
be felt and experienced by the inner Self.
     "During RoHun the inner Self experiences the value of
all four truths in synergy, as one enters his or her own
consciousness and explores the heights and depths. Through
this intimate and fascinating encounter, one is able to
perceive, understand and release through Love and Forgiveness, old negative thought patterns and misconceptions

that have bound one to the wheel of Karma, repeating negative experiences and lifetimes.

"Through the RoHun experience, one is able to reach into the heights of the unconscious and experience Oneness with God, Unconditional Love and a Kinship with all Life. The Sleeping Giant, our Spiritual Being, is awakened and one experiences Self in a new light with a new purpose. One begins to sense living with new direction and understanding.

"RoHun, Love, Forgiveness, Rebirth and Self-Knowledge become a way of life and daily living. A rich resource of creativity flows with an intuitive acceptance to guide one in his or her daily transformations. One becomes who he or she truly is, rather than what he or she does. Life continues with daily challenges, but one perceives differently after RoHun and responds with greater understanding and Love.

"In light of RoHun's ability to carry these major truths to the Inner Man, the more people who are introduced to RoHun, the better. I wish to introduce you to a new idea ... RoHun Enlightenment and Self Healing Cards."

Dr. RoHun continued to channel his ideas of the RoHun Enlightenment and Self Healing Cards that can be used by anyone to gain self knowledge to heal themselves.

Simply called the "RoHun Cards" this unique, copyrighted and trademarked system follows a long tradition of using external objects, such as bones, sticks, coins or playing cards, to gain internal perception.

Many persons reading these words are no doubt already familiar with the use of the Tarot, or perhaps even the Luscher Colour Test, to gain psychological insight.

That the use of such systems, by skilled practitioners, works must be doubted by very few.

The RoHun cards synchronize with the energy of the user so that when they appear in a spread they reflect the actual blocked negative energies, as well as point out in exactly which chakra the block occurs.

In other words, the cards provide insight into where one is blocked in his or her life, the chakra involved, the origin of the blockage (this life or a life previous), the faulty thought pattern that led to the blockage in the first place, and how the blockage may be released.

In brief, the cards provide a quick, easy method of spiritual diagnosis that can be used for self-healing or as part of a preliminary dialogue between RoHun therapist and client.

As the actual process of RoHun is both simple and complex, it is not surprising that the RoHun Cards total 180, and are divided into five color-coded decks, with each deck addressing a different level of understanding and healing.

Without going into great detail as to how the cards are used, which is provided in the instruction manual which accompanies the deck itself, the following will suffice our present understanding, and hopefully entice those interested to obtain the RoHun Cards for their own use!

Deck Number One (The Chakra Card Deck) identifies in which of the seven chakras the blockage occurs and exactly what that block age is inhibiting. An example from this deck might be the drawing of a card which says, "HEART ... LOVE... The block is in your heart chakra and inhibits your ability to love yourself."

Deck Number Two (The Self Card Deck) identifies the Negative Self that has been created as a result of the blockage. In other words, this deck tells us how we think and feel about ourselves as people. For example, we might think of ourselves as an ANGRY SELF or a GUILTY SELF or even a SUFFERING SELF.

Deck Number Three (The Life Card Deck) tells us where, when and how the blockage and this idea of Self came about. Here various archetypes are presented and we learn whether the blockage and this image of Self came from an experience in THIS lifetime or a lifetime PREVIOUS! The various archetypes that are suggested were taken from 'actual' RoHun sessions conducted by RoHun practitioners since the discovery of the process. Most likely you will be as blown away by the insight received from this deck as I was, when I first experienced the cards while visiting Delphi.

Deck Number Four (The Thought Card Deck) identifies the faulty thought pattern, or negative idea, that was crystallized unconsciously and formed into a description of what life is all about. As has already been discussed, this pattern has gone on to create and recreate itself. An example of such a pattern might be, "If I love, people will misuse and abuse it." Besides identifying the faulty thought pattern, an affirmation to clear it is also provided. For the previous example we find this affirmation, "I am free to love. If others want my love, they can have it. If not, they can pass it on to someone who does."

Deck Number Five (The Message Card Deck) gives us a healing message that can be used to replace the negative or faulty thought pattern that has bound us by its psychic chains. This is the fortune cookie at the end of the banquet that enables us to smile and love ourselves a whole lot.

Now that you know something about the actual composition and use of the RoHun Cards, what better way to leave this chapter than by sharing Patricia's insights in her own words:

> We have been looking for a mental approach to RoHun; a way to prepare individuals who have not developed the sensitivity and awareness for RoHun therapy. The cards fulfill this purpose and much more. I recently worked with a woman who had been severely abused as a child and had totally numbed all feeling. It was impossible to do regular RoHun. She had been to many traditional therapists and psychiatrists and had left all of them in anger at their first meeting.
>
> I began her RoHun sessions with the cards. Her first session was two hours working with one block in her brow chakra. She understood the concept of RoHun in that time and built a bond of trust with me. We removed a "Blind self" and the faulty thought pattern, "I am unworthy to be a success." Her next two sessions were incredible. Her clairvoyance was activated after removing the "Blind Self" and she was able to see past lives and recognize faulty thought patterns. After her fourth

session she was ready to go through regular RoHun purification. She began with the three sessions and continued to come on a weekly basis until she reached her goals. She is aspiring to become a RoHun therapist. I couldn't have begun without the cards.

Patricia goes on to say, "The cards educate individuals on the purpose, goals and concept of RoHun. They also prepare an individual's sensitivity, clairvoyance and clairaudience for RoHun as well as build a trust for the more intimate RoHun therapy. Lastly, they easily and simply introduce people to faulty thought patterns, past lives, the continuance of consciousness and the idea of working towards enlightenment."

She concludes by saying, "The healing energy experienced through the use of the RoHun process, while working with the cards, is powerful."

Anyone can learn to use them, and will as a result of their use begin to gain great insight into the workings of his or her own psyche.

Perhaps you, too, may wish to begin your very own RoHun through the use of this most interesting tool!

CHAPTER THIRTEEN

MARCHING TO A DIFFERENT DRUMMER

Great men are they who see that spiritual is stronger than any material force; that thoughts rule the world.
RALPH WALDO EMERSON

If a man does not keep pace with his companions, perhaps it is because he hears a different drummer. Let him step to the music he hears, however measured or far away.
HENRY DAVID THOREAU

Surely, by now you have caught the RoHun fever and the excitement of discovering something new, something special, and something great that could very well be the answer to what you, too, have been seeking to end your own pain and to GET YOUR LIFE MOVING AGAIN!

What yet remains is for us to share the lives and experiences of still other RoHun therapists and students who truly believe that in RoHun they have found the "Pearl of Great Price."

In the biographies and case histories that follow, you will no doubt find one or more persons with whom you truly connect. If, as a result of reading this book you wish to contact a RoHun therapist in your own state or neighborhood, you will find the address and number of the RoHun Institute at the very end of this work.

One word, however, if you decide to do RoHun, DO IT NOW!

Right now, today! Call or write for information. The universe waits for none of us. All your lives are this very moment calling out to you. Will you listen and answer the call?

THE MAN WHO CAME BACK FROM THE DEAD

Of the many RoHun practitioners and students I have met and interviewed, none told a story as unique as that of Daniel Romani who makes his home in Cheektowaga, New York.

Daniel was thirty-six years old at the time "he died." He was going through divorce, had three children, and had just emerged from a bitter seventh month strike at the telephone company where he worked.

For all intents and purposes, his life had followed a normal course ... schools, work, marriage, and now divorce!

But let's let Daniel tell it in his own words...

"Seventeen years ago I had a near death experience. I crossed over and made soul contact. I was in a motorcycle accident going to work. I had just completed a divorce and a seven month strike at work. It was midnight. I was kind of unhappy with my life so I thought I would take the summer off. I had gone to a party and was on my way to work at midnight. It had just started raining. I was going about 80 miles an hour. I slid into a bridge guardrail and went down, seeing everything in slow motion; the hand releasing the accelerator! I was sliding along the ground."

It was here that Daniel paused briefly, and his eyes took on a strange far away look.

He continued his amazing story.

"The next thing I recall was that I was standing, looking down at someone laying there. Someone was running over and kneeling down along side the person who was laying there, but it wasn't me, because I was standing alongside the car with my full body, and all set to go someplace.

"It was midnight and pitch black on the thruway, but I was surrounded with pure light, and was so peaceful. I was all set to go 'someplace' and a voice said, 'Dan. Get Back!'

"I was standing outside the ambulance watching them load 'someone' into the ambulance. Again I was told, 'Dan ... Get back!'

"Again, I don't remember getting back.

"They actually thought I was 'dead.' They had turned my body over because I had lost a lot of blood, shattering the elbow in the left arm and breaking it in three spots. I had also broken and dislocated a wrist, and had lost a finger which was ground up by the guardrail I had hit. I also had a twenty-seven inch gash in my left butt, where I had slid along and also had to have minor surgery on the ankle and the knee."

Once again, Daniel paused briefly before continuing his amazing tale.

He began once again...

"When I was taken to the hospital they took me right to the operating room. I remember being wheeled in. My eyes were closed and yet I could 'watch it,' which was kind of interesting.

"They started working on the hand, and I remember thinking, 'This is wrong. They are not supposed be doing this!'

"Strangely, there was a tingling sensation where the finger was. I remember being a little angry, and got up and sat on the window sill from where I watched the operation on my body taking place.

"Later on, I talked with the doctor who validated what I had seen.

"Again, I was told to, 'Go back.'

"I said, 'No way!'

"Right then, within a flash I was standing in a place in which there were four podiums next to each other. Standing in front of each were four 'beings.'

"We were discussing my life that had just ended, just as you and I are talking right now. There were no judgments ... simply, 'You did this ... You completed this ... You didn't do too well in this.'

"These 'beings' went on to say that since I had just started a self improvement course that was changing my life, I had the choice of going on to the 'School of Wisdom' or returning to the earth plane!

"I don't recall my answer, but I remember waking up the next morning in the hospital with a totally different attitude.

"Within a few months I changed my diet.

"My personality changed.

"I changed all the people in my life.

"Before the accident, I had no purpose to stay here.

"In a way, someone could say that I had 'planned my own suicide!' ..."

Needless to say, Daniel Romani's experience is a most extraordinary one, but as is often said, "When the disciple is ready, the Master will appear."

For Daniel, this Master took the form of his own "death!"

But this is not the end of his story, only the beginning.

While prior to the accident, Daniel had begun seeking his truth through such things as Silva Mind Control and the

Alladin Tape Program, the accident resulted in a total change in his consciousness.   Of this he speaks...

"After the accident, I started reading every night from about 11 P.M. to 5 A.M. the next morning. I read every spiritual book I could find. It was almost like a food that part of me was craving. I just could not get enough of it. Before this, the only thing I read was <u>PLAYBOY</u> or sports magazines! I started out with <u>THE SECRET SCIENCE BEHIND MIRACLES</u> by Max Freedom Long. I was just devouring them. About that same time I met Don Hutter."

For Daniel Romani, Don Hutter was the messenger who first introduced him to RoHun. Don's story will itself be told later on.

Of this more than chance meeting, Daniel says... "I was led to RoHun through Don Hutter. Basically my desire was to learn healing. I retired from the phone company in 1986, after thirty years of service. At that time I chose to dedicate my life to learning and discovering myself. I thought I would only take a three year sabbatical and then decide what I wanted to go back and do. It's been almost 'four' years now."

Daniel continued ... "RoHun was given to me last spring. When I first talked to Patricia on the phone, I told her I wasn't interested in anything called 'mediumship.' She said, 'Well, what are you interested in?' I said, 'Wholeness and seeking the Father within!' Her reply was, 'That's what mediumship is all about!' So I took the mediumship course."

At the time these words are being written, Daniel has long completed his own training as a RoHun therapist.

As a conclusion to our interview, I asked Daniel to say something about what RoHun has meant in his personal search for truth.

He was quick and eager to reply... "For my seventeen years of searching, this is the greatest find. I am so grateful to my Inner Self and Patricia and the creators of RoHun. I think RoHun has the potential to change every aspect of man's nature. Every time we reach in and draw down the RoHunic energy, we are actually giving back, and the RoHun energy is itself growing! It's like as you pour from the pitcher, it is automatically refilled.

"RoHun appears to be very, very pure.

"From what I am learning, this is something that is so beautiful, so pure, so complete that nothing else has to be added."

Thank you, Daniel. We are so happy that you decided to "Get back!"

A FINANCIAL PLANNER MANAGES
SOULS INSTEAD OF STOCKS

Donald Hutter prefers that his friends call him "Doni." He makes his home in Lakeview, New York, not far from Lily Dale.

He holds an MA in Education and spent ten years teaching before entering real estate and financial planning.

Like many others, one of his first introductions to the world of spirit came through the Silva Mind Control course he took in 1973, while still engaged in his real estate business.

Of this training he says.. "I took that to be able to use those abilities TO MAKE MONEY and CONTROL CLIENTS! I had no idea of anything spiritual connected with it whatsoever. It was purely material."

While doing the Silva course, Doni met someone who turned him on to a program called the "ALLADIN TAPES," a series of tape-recorded instructions that worked on the subconscious mind. They were not subliminal but were rather used while one was relaxed.

Of these Doni comments...

"It's a series of very positive programing that forces all the ... to come out! I worked with those tapes for 13 years."

As often is the case, Doni eventually reached a point in his studies where he felt he had reached a plateau. He then turned to hypnosis and past lives regression, for three years, of which he says ...

"I got over the plateau as such, but I later discovered that hypnotic regression is much slower than RoHun. It takes much more time to digest what you experience. You can do in one RoHun session what would take seven or eight hypnotic sessions to accomplish!"

Despite his continued search for Self, he nonetheless continued to feel he had not yet found what he was looking for.

"Every job I did, I felt limited with it, even though I had the education, degrees and so forth."

How did Doni discover RoHun?

"After a year of finally working by myself, I stumbled upon Patricia by pure hunch! My wife and I were sitting around wanting to do something, and the thought came in, 'Go to Lily Dale.'

"So we took a ride down there. I heard Patricia give the lecture at the auditorium.

"As soon as I saw her, I was drawn to her. So I took her seminar, 'The Seven Visions of Self.'

"It wasn't what she was teaching, but what I experienced 'within.' That was the key!

"The next summer, I took another of her courses at Lily Dale and decided to go still further with her.

"During her mediumship class I started working with the RoHun technique called the Cradle, and discovered that I was very natural in using a RoHun process, which I was not yet aware of. It was more intuitive at that point in time than anything else.

"So when I heard of the RoHun class, there were no 'ifs, ands or buts."

Doni's exposure to Patricia's classes convinced him that this was the direction his life should take.

As a result he now spends only part-time at his financial services business, and the rest counseling and helping those in need.

When asked, "Where do you see yourself going?" he replied, "Full time into the healing field. I know that RoHun is going to be a tremendously large part of it. The results I get with clients are absolutely phenomenal!"

Doni was quick to add. "I am convinced that RoHun does in three sessions what it takes a psychiatrist 15 to 20 years to do. With a lot of clients I feel that RoHun goes deeper, because there are a lot of psychiatrists out there who do not believe in past lives! I, personally, cannot see any limitations to RoHun whatsoever."

"What kind of person should consider RoHun as a career?" I asked Doni Hutter.

"You have to have a REAL, not phony, desire to help people. Doing the process is not easy. You have to be more than empathetic with the client. You really have to FEEL for them, because that's how you help them go through their experience. You have to be strong enough yourself to experience what they are experiencing, and yet keep yourself separate from it. You have to be creative. Clients will try avoidance. I have even used such symbolic things as 'bulldozers' and 'cranes' to break through blockages."

And what about someone who might be considering having a RoHun session himself or herself?

"The first thing I would say is don't do RoHun if you like your life the way it is, because it is definitely a life-changing process! There are no IFS, ANDS or BUTS about it!

"Other than that, if you have the desire to change any segment of your life ... Yeah, GO FOR IT!"

Words well said from someone who really knows where he's going!

NOT JUST ANOTHER PSYCHOLOGIST

Kathleen Connors holds a Doctorate in Psychology from the University of Maryland. She lives and works as a psychologist in the Atlanta, Georgia area.

Although she has had countless opportunities to use RoHun, and to evaluate its effectiveness as a therapy, she prefers to speak instead of the dramatic changes it has brought about in her own life.

In fact, one might divide her life into "BR" and "AR"... before and after the RoHun experience!

Before RoHun, there was Gestalt, Transactional Analysis, Group Therapy and Psychoanalysis.

How did she come to RoHun to begin with?

"I heard about it from a friend, who was in the very first class, and had a very dramatic experience with it. She mentioned it to me, and it was right at a time when there was a lot of conflict in my personal life.

"I was taking a cross-country trip with my daughter, who stayed in Texas for awhile.

"While driving back, I had this inspiration to stop in Durham, where Patricia was then based.

"Patricia and I met briefly. I spent the night at her place, and I was intrigued. I wanted to test what it was like as a therapy. So a few weeks later I came back for a weekend, and had a series of sessions.

"It was completely out of the realm of any other therapeutic experience I'd ever had. I was just getting into more metaphysical approaches, including an association I was developing with a massage therapist."

What happened to Kathleen as a result of the RoHun?

"Once I had RoHun on myself I knew what its potential was, and that's what set me up to come and study!"

What kind of person should a RoHun therapist be, I asked her?

"I think the foremost consideration is their capacity to feel. But just having feeling is not enough to make a person a good RoHun therapist.

"The person has to have a 'sense of the play.'

"They have to have the communicative capacity for the verbal processes. They have to be able to identify, not just issues and energies, but the way energies are coagulated into life issues, and played out in a panorama.

"They must be able to move people through the panoramas.

"It very much involves verbal processing, the therapist and the client being able to bring what is happening to a level of external consciousness through verbalization.

"What we are talking about are many dimensions of awareness."

Very serious business, this RoHun stuff, as thought of by Kathleen! What happened to her own practice as a clinically trained psychologist?

"The biggest change in my practice (since RoHun) is in the meaningfulness of it. RoHun has enabled my practice to become a much more existential experience for my clients. It has tremendously elevated what they have been able to get. To date, this has been the most powerful, provocative, transforming therapy I have encountered!"

Strong words from a soft, gentle lady who, as a result of RoHun, will never be quite the same.

THE VOICE AT THE END OF THE PHONE

It is often said that one cannot judge a book by its cover.

I suppose the same thing is true when it comes to a voice on the other end of a telephone!

But when one calls Delphi, the home of the RoHun Institute, the first voice he or she will most likely hear is that of Loryn Martin, who for want of a better title might be called Patricia and Marshall's "GAL MONDAY, TUESDAY, WEDNESDAY, THURSDAY, FRIDAY ... and sometimes SATURDAY and SUNDAY!"

This is the Loryn Martin everyone hears, sees and writes to. But, deep inside there is another Loryn Martin whose own story as to how she came to RoHun is yet another stitch in our Georgia quilt.

Loryn first heard about RoHun from reading "THE GATEKEEPER."

She was living in New Jersey at the time. While still a high school senior, she had read a book by Jess Stern which turned her on to Silva Mind Control.

"After I took that course I immediately wanted to be an instructor, but I was eighteen. When I thought about having to charge people for things, I couldn't do that. So I went on studying myself, just repeating the Silva.

"I also started studying Yoga. I took three different Yoga teacher certifications, and I started teaching that way.

"It was a more gentle way for me to learn to be an instructor. "But my life just put me into situation after situation, until finally it led me back to being a Silva instructor, which I did for six years in New Jersey.

"When I first came to Patricia's I was still teaching Silva.

"It was one of my Silva students who handed me Patricia's book and said, 'You'll like this,' and I did. And later on when I received the information on the school, I knew I would go there."

Like many others before her, Loryn had decided that she didn't like the cold northern winters and would be happier in Florida. She was going to move there with a friend, but somehow her plans were always delayed.

"My first stop on my trip to Florida to scout the area was a week at Delphi for mediumship. I really fell in love with Patricia and the school and the mediumship week had been one of the most transforming experiences in my life. I knew this was what I wanted more of, so I enrolled in the

Internship program, and came back every couple of months to take classes until I graduated and became ordained as a minister in the Church of Wisdom. And then I later enrolled in the RoHun Internship program and became a RoHun Therapist.

"I had heard a lot about RoHun but wasn't sure what it was. Finally, during my fourth visit to Delphi I received my first three sessions plus three sessions of "The Seven Visions of Self" during a RoHun Self Healing week. And I still remember how I felt after that. It was as if my whole being was vibrating with light on many different levels. I felt very ecstatic.

"Also my whole viewpoint on life really expanded. I was impressed very deeply how my thoughts really do create my reality. Oh I knew if I meditated and visualized positive things, it can help to attract those things to me. But RoHun uncovered negative, or faulty, thought patterns that had been hiding deep inside, so deep I had not even been aware they were there. (Thinking back on it, I remember some of these thought patterns would come up as things I would joke around about, never realizing that deep inside I really felt that way..)

"After RoHun I really realized how my beliefs had attracted experiences to me that were related to my own faulty thought patterns. I was grateful to have uncovered and released those beliefs, knowing that I now chose not to hold these beliefs any more, meaning I don't have to attract those experiences to me.

"Many people who aren't really aware of their own thoughts think, 'I don't have anything wrong with me, I don't need RoHun.' Well I think until one reaches enlightenment, meaning unless one, right now is totally God Conscious, totally fulfilled, has total love, abundance, peace, etc. in his or her life, then RoHun would benefit them. Because that's what it does. It uncovers those things that are quite often hidden that are preventing us from realizing our own true nature."

Eventually Loryn did leave New Jersey. After a short stay in Florida, one thing led to another and she ended up relocating to Georgia, and eventually joining the Delphi staff.

What qualities should a RoHun therapist have, according to Loryn?

"Well, probably the most important quality is to really be able to care and want to help others ... the ability to really listen and also to trust in one's own channeling abilities."

Finally, since Loryn is now a fully certified RoHun therapist herself, I asked her to share one of her client's sessions.

"There was a widowed woman left with a teenage son. She had very much loved her husband and he really took care of her. He had been her strength. His death had been very hard on her.

"His image came into the session and they communicated things they never were able to say when he was alive. She could feel him encouraging her to be strong and move forward. There was a whole shift in her energy after that. She had more strength and courage to move forward through her life. It had a profound effect on her. She had had the thought pattern that she couldn't do things without his help, and because she thought that, her life wasn't working out. After the session, she started a new thought pattern that she could do it on her own.

"She was also a woman who liked to help people but something kept holding her back. During the session, she saw herself being accused of being a witch, and being burnt at the stake after helping someone. It helped her to understand the thought pattern she had that if she helps someone, somehow she will get in trouble in the end. Of course she believed it, for things happened like that.

"After the session, she knew things didn't have to be like that anymore. Now she was able to move forward in her life, not only with more strength, courage and self-confidence, but also feeling better about being able to help others."

So the next time you have occasion to call or write Delphi, say "Hello" to Loryn Martin, and know that you are in the good hands of someone who really cares about you ... and RoHun! (Editor's note: at the time of printing, Loryn had moved on to Colorado.)

DOING "COUNTRY" MY WAY!

I can't quite remember when I first heard the lyrics, "How are you going to keep him down on the farm after he's seen Broadway!" but it certainly has meaning when speaking of our next RoHun star.

Jack Bernard Moon now makes his home in Smyrna, just outside Atlanta ... but such wasn't always the case.

"I came from a rural area in northern Indiana. It was hard for my family to accept that someone was 'different' so I hid it for most of my younger years up into my twenties.

"I didn't let it out too often for anyone to know.

"I had an uncle who was very (psychically) gifted, but I wasn't to talk about that!

"I went to a tiny, rural church and attended Sunday school.

"I can recall feeling the emotions of my folks and 'tracking' my Dad when he was in the barn and tool-shed, while I was still in the house waiting for him to come in. I was then just barely walking!"

But fortunately for us, Jack didn't stay down on the farm. "When I moved to Atlanta two and a half years ago, it was kind of funny because then I was exposed to people who said they 'did' psychic things.

"I started to hear people say, 'I do channeling.'

"I said, 'Tell me what channeling is.'

"Well, I was already doing that for years!

"Another one said, 'I cleanse auras.' 'Well, tell me how you do it.'

"Well, I had been doing that for years too!"

So suddenly Jack found that he wasn't so strange, or different, after all.

What he had been doing "naturally," without formal instruction, he now learned had names and was actually "taught."

How did Jack get from the farm to Atlanta to begin with?

"I was almost forced to come to Atlanta. I quit a very good job and started to research various cities. Everything kept saying I had to go to Atlanta.

"I came to Atlanta with no job ... nothing, simply because I knew I was going to grow here. Something about my psychic ability was pulling me here.

I didn't know when or how but I didn't worry about it!"

From Joyce Rennolds, Jack learned of Patricia Hayes and began his RoHun training.

"In the very first or second session, I came out and told Patricia and the group, 'Are you aware that RoHun can affect tissue, and that we can do physical healing with it?'

"What I found is that RoHun was becoming an extension of what my abilities had already established. It didn't compete in any way. It just added to it! It just seemed to be a blending."

Needless to say, Jack has gone on to blend RoHun into his bag of tricks, using everything that works to help and heal people.

"I think RoHun comes from us, really. RoHun is like all the other abilities we have. It's a part of our awareness. Once we quit telling ourselves, 'No, we can't do it!' we become aware that we CAN.

"All our lives we are told, 'No. You can't do this.'

"Suddenly, when we turn around and listen we hear, 'Yes ... Yes ... Yes!' Jack continued.

"When I do a RoHun session, I never know who is receiving the most healing, the client or myself!

"And sometimes I think, 'Hey Moon! Should I be paying THIS person?'

"As I am guiding the client, I sometimes hear myself say, 'Hey Moon, listen to this. Something is talking to you! This applies to you!"

How does Jack think RoHun compares to other therapies?

"In RoHun you see instantaneous results. The other therapies are an ongoing process that has to be reinforced continually. Suddenly you realize that the world is not flat!"

What has doing RoHun done for Jack Moon?

"It has enabled me to help a lot of people become very special. To me it is just a tremendous excitement to watch these people grow... To watch them pop up out of the ground, and the buds come up, and then open into beautiful flowers.

"These people really become aware of themselves. They become aware of the fact that life is a continuum, and that when someone dies they haven't gone anywhere.

"It's not a fear of death. It's that they seem to be racing a clock. Everything has to be absolute, and has to be through infinity. Because they think if they don't get it done this time, they're never going to get through it.

"It's funny, for when they realize that it's a continuum, they also realize that there is no yesterday, today and tomorrow. There is only NOW! Everything is happening currently. So they start to deal with NOW on a NOW basis. Part of RoHun is that it doesn't have to be a painful process."

Why does Jack think RoHun works so quickly?

"RoHun works so fast because the client can 'see' what has taken place. The other forms of therapies are concepts that you have to mentally visualize. People can't always do that. They have to think it through.

"With RoHun, they are in there.

"They are smelling, tasting, seeing."

Does RoHun aid in the individuation process?

"Individuality is 'why' you are so special.

"If you were supposed to be something else, or have a different nose, or a different personality, or a different problem, you would have it!

"RoHun, through its process, accelerates this understanding. It no longer makes you afraid of you.

"Client feedback is the key. First, almost everyone who sees me sends someone else to me. That tells me something. Second, the clients tell me on my recorder, or through little notes, that RoHun has really helped!

"RoHun is something that allows people with the abilities I have to help people without saying, 'OK. I have to spend a big portion of my lifetime learning traditional methods."

As our time to talk was coming to an end, I asked Jack my 'sixty-four' dollar question.

What kind of person should consider becoming a RoHun therapist?

"The person who wants limelight ... the person who wants attention ... the person who wants to be in control and manipulate ... should NOT become a RoHun therapist!

"RoHun is designed for the person who is sincerely interested in helping people grow. If you don't have that person's best interest in mind, don't do it!

"Secondly, RoHun should only be done by someone whom is very comfortable with himself or herself. They should not be looking for distraction, other people's problems, so they don't have to solve their own.

"I also think it is important that a RoHun therapist have a lot of life's experiences. I am not saying that someone young cannot do RoHun, because we do have young people who are doing it, but they have also had a heck of a lot of life's experiences for their age.

"But if people haven't had enough experiences dealing with death, disappointment, abuse problems ... all the things we deal with in our environment ... if you haven't had contact with these things, it is pretty hard to relate to them.

"I don't think that academic training other than the RoHun Institute is necessary, because when you are doing RoHun, you are really NOT doing RoHun. You are channeling the process.

"You are simply allowing the Universe to come in and use you as an instrument, to guide clients into those areas in which they have difficulty, and to help them.

"You are not teaching them anything new, just simply bringing what they already know into their memory, allowing them to see for the first time what was already there for them to see. Intellect has little to do with that.

"You have to have the intelligence to know where they are coming from. You have to have life's experiences to relate to where they are so you can reach them."

ROHUN AND YOUTH

Kimberly Hayes Panisset is a RoHun Therapist, a teacher and mother of two boys and the daughter of Patricia Hayes. I asked her about her younger years.

"In my teenage years I was a rebel. I always felt that I was different than most of my classmates. When I was seven, I was doing psychometry, holding rings and telling people about themselves.

"Every night people were in our home studying psychic and spiritual development.

"I grew up with Arthur Ford, who was like my grandfather, and many other well known people who visited us.

"I thank God for my intuitive and creative abilities. Without them I would have not made it through High School.

"When I was 23 I moved to Calgary, Alberta Canada and began to work with young people. I worked with their energy and taught them how to get in touch with their own creative abilities.

"Integration of one's spiritual, mental, emotional and physical energies is such a necessity in our life. Most people learn how to be smart with their left brain and how to work in a material world without necessarily feeling purpose.

"I found that through my own experience that if you cannot feel purpose, your life becomes empty. We are creators and when you are able to tap into that Cosmic force within, you have the ability to carry out your heart's desires, whatever they may be. We all have a mission and a purpose in this life.

"Young people are far easier to work with because they are not set in their ways. Their resistance is less and once they feel the loving force that is able to flow through them, their fear is quickly forgotten and an inner strength surrounds them.

"Because of my work with youth, many families came together. They began to recognize their children as individuals who also have a need to express their own individuality. I felt a deep sense of purpose from this work as the results were immediately noticeable.

"I feel there will always be tests and challenges in life. No one ever said living on this earth was easy. But when you learn to rely on your inner energy and take those hardships less personally, working through them ... not against them, you become that much stronger on all levels. Integrating all your energies is vital. It leads you to greater feelings of harmony and balance and makes you less connected to the chaos in the world with its mental stresses.

"All this experience and knowledge pushed me to find greater and greater depths of love and understanding, within myself and others, which is what lead me to RoHun.

"When I came back to the United States for a visit, Patricia was experimenting with the techniques Dr. RoHun had channeled. My good timing enabled me to experience this process in its initial stages. I learned so much more about my self in such a short time; I was in awe!

"We both knew we had only touched the surface in this therapy. We knew that as it evolved it would be miraculous by accelerating the time normally needed for one's growth pattern.

"You could feel the depth of RoHun. As it developed more, Patricia put together an experimental group to teach this therapy. I was impressed because of the amount of energy and responsibility it took to teach a process such as this.

"It was not easy. I felt a new hope and inspiration, because I knew many changes would come about now that I had more tools to work with in my life.

"I didn't really become a dedicated RoHun therapist, and teacher of RoHun, until I moved back to the United States. In 1984 I began to work full time at the ROHUN INSTITUTE at Delphi. I was able to consistently work with this process. The results for myself, and the youth I worked with, expanded my own commitment to life.

"In doing RoHun and talking about it, I have visited many parts of the world. People are the same everywhere you go. I think what matters the most in the RoHun process is that you reach the soul of your clients, taking them as far into their greatest as they are able to go! Because of your faith in them, and your love, there really aren't any limits to the process.

"There was a seventeen year old boy who came to see me who was troubled, slow in school, and who had no motivation. His parents were very discouraged. This boy had acne all over his face and a little brown scar on his forehead.

"By the time he came for his third RoHun session, the scar was gone and the acne had almost disappeared. He came for his session feeling proud. You could see the strength he felt; it was beautiful.

"In just that short a time (three sessions), he was able to let go of so many negative feelings about himself. His parents did not understand what had happened. As grateful as they were, they were not aware of energy, or anything relative to spiritual matters, so they too had to come to an understanding within themselves. A new bonding occurred. They were able to begin again with each other at a new level.

"I have worked with many cases like this and the results have always been the same.

"A lot a young people fear they will not be accepted if they don't follow their peers, or do what society tells them. They have not felt any truth, or have any kinship to something greater within themselves. So many get lost in the herd and begin to close off their feelings, thinking they do not matter anyway. So what's the point?

"This attitude creates a hopelessness within. They stop caring and don't try anymore. Negative energies, such as fear, anger, helplessness, or judgement of our world, keep them from living their lives to its fullest.

"I remember one girl. She was very smart in school and active in various groups. She was able to pass herself off as a happy-go-lucky girl to all her peers. When she came to me she was afraid that deep down she was 'bad,' even though she was able to accomplish a lot at school.

"This accomplishment was not real to her. She did not have any feeling of self-worth, or purpose in her life. She felt phoney. We worked specifically with her sense of unworthiness, among other things.

"After the sessions she did not have such a need to participate in all the activities as she had in the past. She became more selective with her friends and began to attract kids that she could trust and knew cared for her. She realized that she was not so bad after all and could let people see her real self.

"When you think about it, isn't that what everyone is afraid of on some level or another? People walk around with their cordial self as a mask, afraid someone might see what is really inside.

"Every human being has beauty and love within. They have qualities that are inherent in each of us that need to be discovered and expressed. Somehow we all get caught in the trivia of everyday living; it stops us from knowing our true self.

"It is an important life goal to search for the 'Self.' Life is not just about being successful in school or work. It is not about being the best. It is more important to do the best you can whatever you do.

"It is important to seek relationships that are healthy and positive, not negative and draining. It is important to move towards feeling more purpose in our everyday existence and to feel balance ... then the ups and downs lessen. This is why RoHun is inspiring to me. It enables us to know ourselves, why we are here. As systematic as this therapy is, it is yet creative and free-flowing and allows us to express the greatest gifts we have. This is love.

"I just remembered a young man who came to me. He had no direction, seemed angry at the world and appeared as if he was under the influence of drugs. This was a challenge because as much as he wanted therapy, he just didn't trust anyone.

"In the first session, I could feel bands of steel around his heart and lower chakras which I broke up. His father had beaten him from the time he was four years old until he ran away from home at the age of sixteen.

"Not only did he have all this anger trapped inside, but he also had taken on his father's anger as well. He hated his father AND himself!

"He expressed, and worked through, a good amount of anger in the first session. He was then able to step back and see his father in a different light.

"His father was suffering, hated life himself ... and as it turned out, had himself been beaten his entire life by HIS father!

"The boy was able to feel compassion because he seemed to understand more about the situation. At this point he was still not ready to let love back into his heart, although he definitely had insight and felt lighter in his body.

"The third session was the true miracle. For the first time he could trust himself enough to let go and feel the depth of love that was in his heart. It poured through every cell in his body releasing all the toxins that had kept him from wanting to be in his body!

"It had never occurred to him that he did have goodness inside and that he WAS able to love. Now he could let his male energy evolve in his own strength. In fact, later on he said he wanted to become a RoHun therapist and dedicate his life to the healing arts.

"Sometimes we ask, 'Why are we the way we are?' Sometimes we blame our parents, or the world, for our feelings of failure. We think the worst about ourselves. We guard our hearts from life and never really experience the true energy of the God within.

"Most people haven't experienced unconditional love. For example, a father loves his son only as long as the son fulfills HIS dreams and becomes a physician. If the son gets out of line, or tries to do what he feels, the father gets angry and threatens to write him out of his will. This is CONTROL ... not love!

"A child learns that if he or she behaves and says the right things, plays the game more or less, then he or she will be loved.

"Kids ask me about God all the time! Is there really a God. Will he punish them for their bad thoughts? Many times this question revolves around their sexuality and things they have done in the past.

"I tell them that God is not easy to explain. You have to be sensitive to the energy of God and feel the essence. God gives life and love gives life. God's energy exists in every-thing that has life. I tell them to become more sensitive by being in nature. Nature has a way of bringing us closer to that God because you can feel its purity.

"I tell them that God doesn't feel judgement towards their mistakes. They are judging themselves, and they can forgive themselves with the love of God that is within. Forgiveness comes from the heart, through understanding only then can you be truly free. God is goodness. For young minds this is simple. Perhaps we have forgotten our simplic-ity through all the complexities in life.

"I teach the kids everyone has the ability to touch another, to help another person. I don't think we were meant to do it all alone.

"We need people in our life at different times to help us through the transitions. This is why I love my work with RoHun. It is not necessary for my clients to see me every week, year after year. After their initial three sessions and seeing them once a month for a skim for about six months to a year, they have already begun to help themselves, and are interested in helping others.

"I watch their progress as their life changes. I help them when they need it and continue to encourage them to be all that they can be."

Kimberly Hayes will have to shoulder more responsibili-ties as RoHun continues to grow. But somehow, in her own way, I feel she is now ready for the challenge. After all, isn't that what "noblesse oblige" is all about?

DOIN'A WHAT COMES NATURALLY

"I have always been a natural psychologist, because I could see clearly what was happening with people."

These are the words of Linda Griffith Bowman who, like many of the RoHun practitioners, cut her teeth on psychology in college.

Currently making her home in Palmetto Point, Florida, Linda got to RoHun through a seminar on spiritual healing that had been offered by the Sufis.

Moving to Florida from New York in 1973, she studied with the Psychic Science Institute in Ft. Lauderdale in 1975.

Her first, real exposure to RoHun came in 1982 through the able hands of Kathy Angeli, herself a RoHun therapist. Linda recalled these sessions for me.

"After the first session I felt a shift in my energy. I felt an opening up, an understanding. The shift consisted of an awareness. All of a sudden, everything started to fit. There was a grouping together."

Linda continued. "I was single at the time, and had just gone through a separation from a man I had been with for eight years. While I understood and forgave, and did all that stuff, I just did it mentally. I didn't know what was wrong. But when I lay down on the RoHun table, all the stuff I never realized was bothering me started to come up.

"Once it came up and was out, I felt a tremendous peace come into my being and understanding.

"I did eight or nine sessions with her."

At the time this occurred, Linda was working as a court reporter, but she was so intrigued by what had happened to her in such a short period of time, she asked Kathy where she could go and study what had taken place.

Linda was quick to call the school and spoke to Patricia personally.

"The first training course just changed my life. I got the keys to stay conscious. At this time RoHun was out of its infancy, but still crawling. It was a toddler at that point.

"I started right off with RoHun and loved it. The first year out after my training I did about thirty to forty clients. It was a natural calling for me."

Needless to say, Linda took to RoHun as a duck takes to water and went on to become a very active RoHun practitioner. "By now I have done close to 100 cases. It is my feeling that someone starting RoHun should go for the first three sessions in three consecutive days, come back in a month, and then continue once a month for another three months.

"For real dedicated growth, the person should return at least once every six months."

What does Linda think of RoHun as compared to other therapies?

"Anyone who is in any other therapy has found that RoHun is the quickest!"

I asked Linda to share a few of her most interesting cases.

"I had a case that was really incredible. It was man who had been in two plane crashes. He was a pilot. He was in his 40's. He came with pins in both his legs.

"When he was on the table and I was working with him, any plane that came by did something to the metal in his legs. So he was all over the table.

"His wife and daughter had pushed him to come to me.
"He had come because his life wasn't working. He and his wife had separated because he was very controlling.

"When he was supposed to come for the third session, he became totally catatonic, and I got his phone call. I told his daughter, 'Just bring him in. Don't talk to him, just bring him in.' I laid him down and just took charge.

"He went into a past life, and saw himself as a woman who went into a field, picked mushrooms and unknowingly poisoned her entire family. She was not aware that the mushrooms were poison.

"It was an accident, but the guilt was there.

"In this lifetime, he had accidentally killed a wife in a plane crash, and had guilt from this as well. It was a pattern.

"He had been living with the guilt of what happened to his wife in that plane.

"I can't tell you whether a past life is factual or created, but it lives in the person, or universal consciousness, or archetypes!

"I am not into labeling. I am into moving the energy from wherever it's stuck.

"As a result of his realization, he was able to forgive himself.

"This was the most complicated case I have ever worked with because it was so traumatic."

I asked Linda to share still another case she thought would be of interest.

"Another case was a young woman, age 38, who had continual female problems, and was struggling with the issue of intimacy.

"She never understood why she had a lot of fear and could not trust men. She fabricated all kinds of female problems so she really could not become intimate.

"What came out was a previous life in which she had been sexually and physically used and abused, and never understood why it was. It was somewhere in the Middle East. She was one of many, like a harem situation, but really abused.

"Today she is married. Within a month after the RoHun, her physical problems began to clear up. So serious were her problems before RoHun, she was going to go for an operation, having been diagnosed as having a possible malignancy in the ovaries. This cleared up totally!"

Who can really say why they are led to choose one vocation over another?

Thoreau would have us believe that the majority of us lead lives of quiet desperation, most likely due to our being in the wrong place, wrong career, wrong relationship, etc.

For Linda Griffith Bowman and others, RoHun was the means to find out once and for all what they should be doing with their lives!

Isn't this something each one of us needs?

REAL ESTATE TO ROHUN

I first met Steven Feder at Delphi in December, 1989.

I was intrigued by him; because in between classes, he seemed to be spending as much time on the telephone as I was!

Steven is a self-made, highly successful entrepreneur

who has been involved in business for twenty of his forty years.

In 1986, he sold his various real-estate companies and made a conscious decision to take some time off and explore.

On reading a book by Allan Cohen, whom he discovered he had gone to college with, he learned that Allan made his home in Maui, so off he went to the Islands seeking a personal meeting with the author.

By chance, while visiting Maui, he met a friend who turned him on to RoHun.

But Steven was no complete stranger to the world of the mind, for although his life centered on business, he had done the well known EST training, as well as its successor, THE FORUM, when he was thirty-three.

EST had a tremendous impact on Steven, so much so that I asked him to compare his experience with it to that of RoHun.

"RoHun is much gentler than EST. It transcends it in a number of ways. First, it gets you to take a close look at your negative faulty thought patterns, but it also gets you to take a close look at what you can replace them with!

"EST and the FORUM dealt more with getting the negativity out, and there was very little transcendence of that, and getting to the positive replacement of it all.

"RoHun also comes from a much deeper quality of the heart than EST and the FORUM did. It is much more spiritually profound than EST was.

"EST was about sharing in public whereas RoHun is a one on one sharing with a qualified therapist you can trust.

"In EST you were asked to trust 200 persons you never met before. EST was a nice introduction ... a kind of shock for me! The follow-up in EST, the various seminars, just dealt with the same issues in a different light.

"With RoHun, the advanced techniques really peel off the layers, one after the other, on a deeper and deeper level, so you keep getting more and more insight into the whole thing!

"In EST, I didn't like the fact that everyone sounded like robots. The vocabulary was 'robotic.' You could walk into a room and know who was doing EST, and who wasn't, by what words they were saying in ordinary conversation!

"I have had enormous transformation in my life through RoHun!"

As of this writing, Steven has been certified as a RoHun therapist.

Before either he or I had to run off to the telephone, I asked him what he thought were the main qualities of someone who wanted to become a RoHun practitioner.

"RoHun therapists should have sensitivity, perception, the ability to relate heart to heart with people, and a background of knowing themselves exceedingly well before they commence.

"They have to be ready to move forward with their lives, and not be struggling with their own problems."

At this point the telephone rang. I can't quite remember whether the call was for Steven or myself. But our talk came to an end, anyway!

A SOCIAL WORKER DISCOVERS ROHUN
AND HEALS HERSELF TOO!

There is always a certain excitement about being part of something BRAND NEW! It's like moving into a freshly painted apartment, or using a new suitcase for the first time, or that special smell that comes with a new car!

To the many RoHun students and therapists I have met, there is certain commonalty that causes their eyes to light up, and their faces to strike a smile when they talk about Delphi and RoHun!

I guess its because they are really a part of something new, and something truly great!

One such RoHun fan is Nancy McTavish who lives in Dunkirk, New York, and who works as a social worker.

Nancy first heard about RoHun through our friend, Don Hutter, while attending church at Lily Dale. As a result of Don's insistence, Nancy took the mediumship course which Patricia was then teaching at Lily Dale.

"After I had taken the Mediumship, that was as far as I was going to go. That was it! I was firm! There was no intention of going any further. First of all, I didn't have the time. Secondly, I didn't have the money. That was it, I was not going to do it.

"But I kept having this feeling, 'Here it is. This is what you are supposed to do. This is how you are going to do it. This is how you are going to get there!"

Needless to say, Nancy was having the well-known battle of knowing what she had to do to change her life, but not wanting to change.

Gee, where have we heard that before?

Fortunately for Nancy, and for us, Dr. RoHun had his way with her!

"The first time I came down here (Delphi) for RoHun, I remember saying to Kimberly and Patricia, 'I don't know why I am here. I really don't.'

"But for some reason, I had to be here. It's an emotional thing ... I'm going to cry. It was an emotional thing then and it still is!" Why was Nancy led to RoHun to begin with?

"I think, in retrospect, it was for my own healing, so I could go on to help someone else.

"I had had a reading a year ago from a woman who said she saw me doing 'psychic surgery,' which were the words she used. I thought, 'Sure ... I believe in this, but there is a limit to how much I believe!'

"So I still wasn't accepting, and the first week I was down here, they were talking about psychic surgery. All of a sudden the two clicked!" But besides helping Nancy find a 'new' Nancy, RoHun also helped heal a twenty year bout she has had with interstitial cystitis.

"After I had the RoHun, it was the first time I can remember being pain free. The medical treatments I had had before, they said would help the bladder; but the pain was still there.

"Suddenly the pain, the pressure, and the frequency began to disappear. Now I am not taking any medication.

"The problem first came after a period of stress, and many changes in my life.

"I think I have just been releasing a whole lot of frustration and anger, a lot of things.

"And my relationship with my brother, with whom I haven't spoken to for seven years, has also improved as a result of the RoHun."

How would Nancy compare RoHun to traditional psychotherapy?

"This is more intense, deeper and quicker. With the others you just sit and talk and have a conversation. You talk but you really don't get anywhere. It was just talking, talking, talking.

"But with RoHun, you look at things, you see things. You look and you forgive yourself, and other persons too, for what you perceived their action was. What they thought they were doing might not have been what you saw at all!"

I asked Nancy how it felt to be pain free after twenty years.

"It's a wonderment. I feel my life for this past twenty years was adjusted around my disease. The other day I left home, went shopping, had lunch and didn't have to run to the john, having been gone for five hours!"

Our time was running out, so I asked Nancy one final question. How would you sum up what RoHun has done for you?

"For me it has given another opportunity to live, to be a whole person, to have a better quality of life ... Living and not just existing! I feel that this is just starting, and it's so overwhelming. It's as if the whole world is opening up. There's a whole, big, wonderful world out there. Now I am going to get a chance to look at it. It was there before, but now I am looking at it differently."

As these words are being written, Nancy McTavish is fast approaching the time when she can retire from her day job, having put in twenty years of service.

When we last spoke, she talked about going back to school and getting that degree she put on the back burner, as many of us have done, in order play wife and mother.

We are sure that whatever Nancy does in the future; RoHun will be an important part of it.

AN APPLE FOR THE TEACHER

"Everything in my life since RoHun, as I look back on it, has been pulled together by golden threads!"

With these words we begin the story of Sandra Phillips Ballard, who currently resides in Sapphire, North Carolina.

"I can look back over this whole process and see that when I began to listen to my intuition that told me to go down to see Patricia, that told me to take the RoHun, all things began to unfold."

Sandra's story could belong to any prim and proper girl raised in the South.

While early on in life she realized that she had a desire to learn, and was unlike the rest of the family, she none-the-less followed its deep traditions. She joined the Baptist Church, went to Converse College where she earned Bachelor's and Master's degrees in Education, got married, got divorced, got remarried, had three children, and proceeded to die inside!

"I got married out of fear of my own passionate nature. I had tried to fit the mold of what the '50's Woman' was to be, and bring children in, which was the highest form of spiritual awareness I could know at that time!"

Sandra turned to reading everything and anything to find out what life was really about.

"Fortunately, one day in my twenties I realized that there was no truth except what was within me, and that I would never be able to agree with any of them. That was the day I began to evolve faster."

After locking horns with the Baptist Church, she reached the decision that it and her first marriage had to go!

A second marriage brought her three children; but after seven years, it too came to an end.

Her children grown, Sandra was on her own once again.

A friend told her about Patricia Hayes' school, and she recalls thinking, "I need to do this if possible."

After a few false starts, she did do it and went to Patricia's, with great expectations. There she met three friends who had come to study together ... a time management specialist, a Yale Divinity School graduate working on a doctorate, and the wife of a psychiatrist.

All three told her that RoHun "had changed their lives so dramatically, there was nothing in their lives that touched it!"

Still even stronger were the comments of the psychiatrist's wife who said, "It will do more for you in three sessions than three years of psychiatry, and I know because I have been there. And, I am also married to a psychiatrist!"

Given this kind of recommendation, Sandra had little doubt that RoHun was something she wanted in her life.

But in order to take the year long RoHun training, she had to take time off from her teaching duties in order to attend the four training sessions.

Although it was not normal for permission for "time off" to be given, she submitted a written request to do so, and much to her surprise received a hearty 'Yes.'

Surely, this was another sign from the heavens that she was doing the right thing!

After her RoHun training in September, 1986, while driving home, she had an unusual experience she will never forget.

"It surprised me as I was riding back through the mountains in the rain. All of a sudden it was as if a veil was taken off my eyes. Suddenly I could see who I was, where I needed to go in life, and what I had to do to get there. And I just laughed. It was as if the energy just shifted into 'Go.' Just as this happened, the rain stopped and a double rainbow appeared in the mountains. I felt like I floated all the way back."

The rest of our story is history.

Sandra is no longer teaching high school but she is still teaching! She is also going full steam ahead as a RoHun therapist, and travels and gives lectures on RoHun throughout the country.

Because of her reputation as a healer extraordinare, I asked her to share some of her most significant cases.

"Robert was a young man who had gone through two divorces. During the first session, he began to twist and turn as if he was going to roll off the table. I realized that he had an extreme blockage in his lower chakra.

"I asked him to let go of this and let the energy flow upward. He told me that he couldn't talk about this, because if I knew why this was happening, I wouldn't love him.

"I assured him that this was not the case, and that anything that had happened in his life was for his growth and spiritual development, no matter how he may have perceived it.

"He proceeded to relive an experience that occurred when he was only eight years old. He had been drawn down to the bayou by a number of older boys, and while there had engaged in various sexual acts that he later found displeasing.

"To appease his guilt, he had climbed a tree and thrown himself down thirty feet onto a steel spike in the ground, attempting to kill himself. Fortunately, his would-be suicide failed, and he only succeeded in knocking the wind out of himself.

"Nonetheless, thinking himself dying, he crawled through a hedge to a nearby church where he found a drinking fountain, previously unknown to him, from which he drank in order to restore his breathing.

"We then moved ahead in time, and he described his attempt at various sexual experiences in his adult life, which were never consummated.

"He and I worked through this experience as simply the typical search to 'Know Self.' He forgave the various boys, as he pictured them one by one.

"He came to realize that his Fundamentalist religious background had caused him to perceive this experience as 'sin.'

"Once he realized that climbing the tree was an attempt to reach God, and that his crawling to the church was symbolic of his forgiveness, he burst into laughter and was freed.

"In later sessions he was able to trace the effects of this experience.

"At the end of the therapy, he picked me up and swung me around and said, 'My God, Sandra, If I had known this I would never have gone through two divorces!'"

I asked Sandra for another case she recalled.

"Laura was a young lady who came to me believing that she had killed her mother who died when Laura was seven. Regressing her to that age we found that that was not the case, and so moved her back in time to when she was three.

"She was standing in the kitchen pulling on her mother's apron, and was told by her mother, 'Go away. Leave me alone.'

"She then turned and thought, 'She doesn't love me. I don't love her.' So the 'emotional murder' had occurred at that point.

"I took Laura still back further into the Light and had her express why she was born into this family and had chosen this mother and father to realize her own power.

"After this I brought her back into the womb, and she began to realize that she did not have to fear being born, as the energy she felt was her mother's and not her own.

"She was taken to her moment of birth and asked to look into her mother's eyes. She said, 'My God. She did love me' and started crying.

"We then went back into her mother's past, to the time her mother was five, and saw that she was a delicate, artistic child who had been killed in her own environment. This was why she was so cold to her daughter later on.

"In other words, it was her mother and not herself who chose to die at age five!

"What Laura had done was to tune in to her mother's pain and her desire to die, and take it on as if it was her own. Hence, when her mother did die two years later; she believed she had 'killed' her. She and her mother embraced, and forgave each other and let go.

"Laura's alcoholic ex-husband, whom she had married while she was in college, was found in her heart chakra. They had divorced in great pain, and he later died in a ditch from alcoholism. She brought him back, went back with him to when he was 'five' and saw what had shaped his development. They in turn embraced and forgave each other and Laura was free."

How about another one, I asked Sandra.

"I met Barbara in Minnesota at a workshop I was giving. She came up to me during the break and said, 'Yesterday I had a test run and I have the first stages of melanoma. During the night I had a dream of a serpent, and today while you were speaking of the chakras as a serpent, a light hit me. I know you are the one to help me. I want to work with you as quickly as possible!'

"By coincidence, my father had died from multiple melanoma, which fact I shared with her the next day, which I interpreted meant I had a strong connection with her. We talked and she cried and said, 'I know you are the one to help me.'

"She couldn't wait to get started. Once we did, I experienced some of the most powerful RoHun sessions I have ever dealt with. Her energy was so passionately designed to live. It had gusto and vehemence, reminding me that each person is his own healer.

"Those of us who call ourselves healers are only instruments for the healing force to come through. Hence, she was actually healing herself. By the last session, she had let go of many things in her life so we were ready to work with her physical energy.

"I worked pouring columns of light, through her crown chakra into every cell in her body. And she could feel it. We could feel this dark energy coming out of her which was just pouring out.

"I left for home the next day but was in contact with her periodically. Each time she went to her physician, the melanoma was found to have dropped in count.

"About six months later, I saw her again. She rolled up her sleeve to show me signs of blotches on her skin.

"She said, 'These blotches came out six months ago after my last session in which the energy just poured through me. The day after that session, all the toxins began to pour out of my body.'

"We hugged each other and laughed. I said, 'Isn't it wonderful that ugliness is beautiful!'

"To my knowledge, her count has continued to go down, and I am hopeful that she will experience a complete remission."

It may be said of Sandra Phillips Ballard that she has indeed found the pearl of great price through RoHun.

Perhaps you, too, can become so fortunate!

A PHYSICIAN'S DAUGHTER FINDS A BETTER WAY

When I first interviewed Meg Latham Gamble at Delphi last December, she had that very special glow that throughout history only 'mothers-to-be' possess.

In fact as I saw her actively participate in various RoHun sessions and demonstrations, I began to wonder what her soon to be born child might say some day about her 'own' pre-natal experiences!

Meg, herself, is certainly unusual since she is the daughter of not one, but two, physicians. Her father died when she was only twelve.

"My father was a very interesting man. He was my best friend when I was growing up.

"I was an unusual child as by the time I was eighteen months old I was speaking, singing and saying my 'ABC's. I was unusually advanced for my age. Since then I have come to know that my father and I worked together on many, many levels. He was my teacher throughout many lifetimes.

"He was a super genius. He was not only a medical doctor. He was fascinated by all kinds of things.

"I remember him sitting me down and telling me about time warps, black holes and how the universe works.

"He died from a fatal blood clotting disease, something like phlebitis. He really needed to go and passed away when he was only 42.

"So that was my beginning with these things."

While these early memories were Meg's initial quest, her interest in the unusual, which began when she was a child, continued into her teens and adult life.

"I had seen several ghosts while growing up. I saw a UFO when I was fifteen.

"I have been studying in this field, seriously, for about thirteen years, but it just scares my mother to death.

"My mother is a doctor, too, a pediatrician, and very straight. She is more by the book, prim and proper. She is just now saying she read a book, Richard Bach's, and talking to me about crystals and asking me a couple of things."

After completing high school, Meg went to the Art Institute in Atlanta, which is a school for commercial art. While there, she fell in love with a Las Vegas musician who was passing through and with whom she later went on the road.

"It was something I had to do. I not only got to visit a lot of places, but I lived in a lot of places, too. Eventually, the group broke up and I came back to Atlanta."

It was only after her return to Atlanta that she finally admitted her interest in the paranormal.

"I was studying for a long time, and it was very important to me because it was real. But it also scared me a little bit.

"I read books. I studied on my own. I had friends who were involved. I did meditation. I did hypnosis on my own and was always out in nature by myself.

"While I knew I had seen ghosts and UFO's, I didn't want to share this with too many people!

"I had been living on the road for about four and a half years, and then came back to Atlanta. I worked at Saks Fifth Avenue, never having worked in retailing before. After about six months, a lady who had heard about my abilities asked me to come and manage her store, a boutique. She needed a manager, a buyer, etc.

"Well, she came to me and said, 'I like you, but need to know if we are of like minds.' She had just gotten through taking Patricia Hayes' Mediumship course, which in those days was called 'Discovery.'

So it was in 1979 that Meg began a journey which has lasted all this time. Referring to her connection with Patricia, and the school, she is quick to comment.

"I feel if anybody is involved, they have to be realistic. It's very important that you are able to integrate it on all levels. That's what keeps me working with the school."

As of this writing, Meg has conducted about fifty RoHun sessions. I asked her to describe her 'own' first RoHun session.

"Absolutely phenomenal!! The difference between Ro-Hun and anything else you do is very personal. My bottom line for RoHun is that it is a miracle of self.

"Until you are your 'self,' you are not an equal to anyone else. You will not attract to you what's right for you, because you are not 'who' you really are! We all think that we are one thing and attract on that level. And when we go through our changes, we are in the 'wrong' place with the 'wrong' people!

"RoHun has been a miracle in my life, physically as well. I was supposed to be crippled two and a half years ago; I had a terrible accident when I was twenty-one.

"Since RoHun, I have only been to the chiropractor twice in the last two years."

Sometime after my interview with Meg, I learned that she delivered a beautiful daughter. One day I am sure she will ask her mother, 'What were you doing in Delphi during ten days in December, 1989!'

I can't wait to hear Meg's answer!

TWO SISTERS DISCOVER ROHUN

One of the greatest joys I have had in my life has been counseling people and watching them "grow."

In fact, it is my cherished belief that we do not <u>go</u> through life but rather <u>grow</u> through it! In looking back, I have certainly done my share of growing! How about you?

While at Delphi, I had the unexpected pleasure of meeting and speaking with two sisters, Judith Herzog and Renee Harel, who currently reside in Edgewater, New Jersey.

Although when viewed separately each possesses unique talents, after seeing them together, it is hard to picture them apart.

For this reason, I like to think of them as RoHun's "Dynamic Duo" ... you know, like a Batman and Robin!

But let me first tell their story, and then you can decide for yourself if I am right.

We will begin by letting Renee, the older of the two, go first.

At the time Renee discovered RoHun, she had just gotten married for the second time. As she did not have to work, she suddenly found herself with time on her hands, a dangerous position to occupy!

"I was out of work for the upteenth time. I was not going back any more to something I did not enjoy doing.

"I had started as a teacher and then went into restaurant management, and then was very disillusioned. I went into acting and advertising sales, although my degree is in art education, because I had to get a degree in something!

"I always had an inner searching that there had to be something I would enjoy doing that wasn't 'work.' People around me said, 'You are nuts ... crazy. Work is work and you have to hate it!'

"But with me, when I didn't like something, I would get up in the morning, without anything behind me, and leave and go on to the next thing!"

How very familiar is Renee's story; but let's let her continue.

"For the first time in my life, I didn't have to work. From week to week, I was going from bookstore to bookstore and reading. I came across a copy of THE GATEKEEPER at a little occult bookstore in Edgewater, New Jersey. It was the last book on the last shelf.

"I went and read it on my honeymoon!

"So that led me to Patricia Hayes."

To make a long story short, Renee went and took the RoHun training and is now a certified RoHun therapist.

"Every day I wake up and say, 'I want more RoHun,' and the phone rings and I do readings. I feel like my life has finally found where I am supposed to be.

"There is so much greater understanding between my parents and myself. It's as if whoever I touch, in some way 'they have been RoHuned!' In their eyes, I am making money ... but more important, I am happy!"

As of this writing, Renee, who just received her RoHun certification, has done RoHun therapy with about fifteen persons. Most of these she worked with are middle to upper middle class professionals, lawyers, accountants etc. whom she describes as "main stream materialists."

I asked her to share one of her cases.

"One case was very interesting ... an accountant, in his 50's, married, three children.

"He only had three sessions but his backaches disappeared completely.

"He also just went away with his wife for the first time; she called to tell me. He's an accountant and always pinched pennies. This trip with his wife was a life changing thing for him!

"I had still another client who had candida, and it's now gone. She had been abused by her mother, and she allowed other people to use her."

I asked Renee where she saw the whole RoHun thing going.

"Big time ... Big time! This is my life!"

So there you have her story in a nutshell.

But wait a minute, what about Judith?

Here's how she tells it...

"My sister, Renee, came back from the mediumship course and said a few important words to me about what she had learned about herself. Namely, that she was very controlling! "'I don't need to do this to you anymore, Judy,' she said! "I said, 'Let me see this book!'

"She added, 'The next mediumship course is next month.'

"I went right to the RoHun!"

Sisters, sisters, sisters ... my how they interact. But Judith, like her sister, has still more to say.

"I had always thought of myself as intelligent, a go-getter, and had a lot of drive. But my life, I always thought of as a whirlpool. Just as I would reach the top I would fall down again. My relationships with men and my career was always changing. I had so many professions, and lots of relationships, but I wasn't happy.

"I had all the self help books, and was always looking and searching and being open to criticism about myself. So when I saw what RoHun had done for Renee I said, 'I have to go for this.'

"It was wonderful for me and was very powerful. I had already been involved with astrology and other spiritual things for about fifteen years. I started with Silva Mind Control when I was about 23 years old.

"I have a sales and marketing background. I also went to acting school and then to broadcasting school."

So what's happened to Judith as a result of her RoHun experience?

"In the short time I have studied RoHun, my life has already changed because I was ready. I was hungry! In one session, you will see what happens. It's so amazing and it's like magic. Whoever you are, and whomever I work with, once they have one session, there's no controlling it! Your own life, the people in your life (even if they don't live near you), they are activated! I have seen every one of them, and what has happened, because they come back. I am NOT a Guru. I am a channel!"

Again, my sixty-four dollar question. What qualities should a RoHun therapist have?

"I think the most important thing to realize is that you are a 'channel.' Then you can really put out of the way the 'Judy', or whoever you are, and just say, 'Use me!'

"The most important thing is that you stay in your heart!"

Well said, Judith and Renee.

We all expect bigger and better things from the both of you.

But more important ... You both expect the same!

A MODERN MADAME DE FARGE CHOOSES ROHUN

One of my favorite scenes in all literature is from Charles Dickens', A TALE OF TWO CITIES, in which Madame De Farge is always portrayed knitting (while she utters various social comments much like a Greek chorus) as the plot thickens.

I first met Poochie Myers, who now makes her home in McCaysville, Georgia, in Key West where she also has a home.

She is an artist in various mediums, including knitting, in which she excels greatly, and which she teaches from time to time.

Living in Key West, Poochie has long been friends with Renate Perelom and Emmy Chetkin, with whom she has shared many things, including The Course in Miracles, Rebirthing and Reiki.

While visiting Lily Dale, Emmy turned her on to Patricia's upcoming course in Mediumship and the rest is history.

"Two or three days into Mediumship there was mention of the word RoHun, and all I knew was, 'I'm going. I'm not going to be in Lily Dale, I'm going to be there (Delphi)!'

"Then RoHun comes along ... I don't know what will come next!"

What's Poochie going to do now that she has added RoHun to her already full bag of tricks?

"I don't know what I am going to do next. I know one thing, I am not going to make any plans; because I know better. I now just keep moving, going. I see myself giving lectures on RoHun or different ways to enlighten yourself!"

What has RoHun done for Poochie, herself?

"Finally, I have feelings. This lifetime when I chose to be born, I was a 'split baby.' I came in and took a look and said, 'No way. I am leaving my feelings out of here because things are not right!'

"Also in Rebirthing, the same issue kept coming up ... to get rid of my mother energy. I thought I had gotten rid of my mother and was so proud of myself, until I had RoHun.

"To have feelings for the first time in this lifetime is fantastic. I had no compassion, because I could not feel.

"I think RoHun is fabulous. And I think it is a major breakthrough for psychiatrists. It will probably take 200 or 300 years before they get around to accepting it, however. But since everything is so much faster now, perhaps it won't take long!"

Thanks for sharing, Poochie. We think you are fabulous, too!

WHAT GOES AROUND COMES AROUND!

In the introduction to this work I made mention of the fact that in actuality it was Renate Perelom, herself a RoHun practitioner, who first introduced me to the work of Patricia Hayes.

Renate has a BA in Education and spent her early years teaching elementary school. In addition, she holds certifications in Neuro-Linguistic Programing (NLP) and Reiki.

Renate began studying RoHun and became certified as a RoHun therapist. I asked her to share a few of her most unusual cases.

"This was a woman in her mid 40's who had been referred to me by another client.

"To the outside world she appeared successful in her career.

"Her inner life, however, was ravaged with pain, anger and guilt which had produced symptoms of depression, suicidal tendencies, and emotional fragility.

"If this was not enough to deal with, in an attempt to ease her inner pain, she had become a closet cocaine addict.

"In the RoHun sessions, she revealed that her sister had been raped by her uncle, while she had been in the house, as the source of her guilt for not speaking out!

"In addition, incest issues with her father emerged, and the image of a mother who was in total denial came out.

"By tuning into her parents, she understood the loss of Self her experience with her parents had taught her.

"If this hadn't been enough, she had gone on to have an affair with a co-worker and later discovered herself pregnant.

"Once again to hide her guilt, she claimed the child was her husband's, thereby betraying her son, herself, her husband and the real father!

"As a result of her realizations from the various RoHun sessions, she placed herself in a cocaine rehab center, resolving to break her addiction. She wrote letters to her parents and others, forgiving them and expressing her newly found love and gratitude.

"These extraordinary changes came after only three RoHun sessions and one skim session."

I asked Renate to share another case.

"This was the case of a married man, in his mid 30's, who was totally unable to feel any joy and peace.

"He spent all his time just doing things, and always had to be in control. One of his complaints was that he could not draw healthy people into his life.

"For many months now, he had been going to a chiropractor three times a week because of extreme lower back problems.

"During the very first RoHun session, much to his surprise, he returned to the moment of his birth. Immediately after he was born, he relived being placed aside, as an unexpected twin sister had been born, much to the surprise of his mother and the doctor!

"For the first time, he experienced feelings of abandonment as a baby together with anger, jealousy and rejection.

"As a result of these feelings, he had early on thought that in order to be acknowledged, he had to be better than anyone else, totally in control of every situation, a super-achiever, and that all women (i.e., his twin sister) could not be trusted!

"We went back to the doctors, mother, and sister. For the first time he realized his sister did not choose to manipulate or take away from him, only to share in life!

"Although he had not spoken to his sister for six years, he immediately called her after the first session to share his new understandings.

"After the third session, he was able to start jogging as his back pain was no longer there."

The next case Renate shared really struck home. The client was a Viet Nam veteran who after the war found himself unable to sleep without medication. In time, his inability to sleep had led him to use a combination of valium and cocaine!

"During the war he had killed many soldiers and civilians. After awhile he found himself unable to tell the difference between the two.

"In his Root Chakra, he looked into the eyes of the enemy and saw only suffering and the desire to survive. In a way, he had created an enemy within himself!

"He looked into the eyes of humanity and wanted to experience no separation. He looked at himself as a soldier and saw only duty and the love of country.

"After three RoHun sessions, he was able to sleep without drugs.

"As a result of his experience, he decided to help counsel, and be available for other Vets."

Strange, powerful magic is this RoHun stuff!

Before I finished talking with Renate she shared with me a letter she received dated October 1985, in which a client expressed, in her own words, what RoHun meant to her. So rich is this letter, it rightfully serves as a fit ending to this chapter; hopefully convincing anyone who may still have doubts as to the effectiveness of RoHun to change lives.

"When I came for RoHun therapy, I did not know what to expect, although I knew I had been drawn there for a reason!

No one on earth, except perhaps Renate, could know what I was going through.

I felt mistrust, betrayal, depression, anxiety, fear and had really started to wonder if death would not be a safer place to be.

After experiencing three sessions of this therapy, I am a new person; I am me.

Each session brings a new experience, a new awareness, a new energy until your physical, mental and spiritual awarenesses are cleared of all the garbage life has stored up.

You actually feel you have given birth to yourself. You are one with the Universe.

Try it ... You'll love it!

J.R."

CHAPTER FOURTEEN

THE DELPHI DREAM

239

The most celebrated oracle was at Delphi, on a slope of Mount Parnassus. Surrounding boulders gave back a wondrous echo; vapors emanated from a natural grotto, and in a crypt stood the image of Apollo, framed by laurel. When the oracle was to be rendered, the Pythia, sitting on a golden tripod, moved closer to the steaming crevasse. Soon she was overcome by a divine delirium-her neck swelled, her body writhed in convulsions, her head jerked violently. The crisis was shocking enough to fill all who beheld her with religious awe.

...Kurt Seligmann, MAGIC, SUPERNATU-
RALISM and RELIGION, p. 91

What's really in a name?

If you believe in the mystical teachings, the answer to this question is simply, "A lot!"

So it is no wonder that Patricia Hayes and Marshall Smith have chosen to 'name' the international headquarters for the RoHun Institute in McCaysville, Georgia, "DELPHI," after what was perhaps the most famous oracle of Apollo located on the southern slope of Mt. Parnassus in Greece.

It was here, for over a thousand years, that priestesses called Pythia delivered prophecies and answered petitioners' questions while in self-induced trancelike states.

But what really IS an "oracle" anyway?

The word itself comes from the Latin oraculum, "a little mouth thought to produce the still, small voice of destiny."

In other words, what we are talking about is PROPHECY, which the philosopher Plato called "the noblest of arts."

But to the ancients, oracles meant not only the actual words or prophecies spoken, but the place itself in which the deity or inspired person delivered his utterance!

In fact, so great was the Greek belief in the value of such prophecy that Socrates called it, "the special gift of heaven, and the source of the chief blessings among men," maintaining that it "conferred great benefits on Hellas, both in public and in private life."

Unlike the Jews, Christians or Moslems, the ancient Greeks had no sacred writings from which to glean practical guidance to solve life's problems. While the Greek poets were held to have been inspired by the various Muses, or demi-gods, such did not make their poetry 'God's word.'

Further since it was the function of the priests to simply conduct public worship, mainly through the offering of sacrifices to the various gods, rather than delivering sermons or hearing confessions, the need for divining the will of the gods remained.

In time, however, such a need was filled by the introduction in some temples (mainly dedicated to Apollo) of oracles, men or women who had been placed in trance and who would answer questions from their subconscious minds.

In historical times, Apollo was worshipped by all the Greeks as the son of Zeus, king of the gods, and Leto.

Apollo was the god of prophecy and patron of poetry, music, medicine and the healing arts. After the 5th century B.C., he was also identified with the sun and called Phoebus Apollo — 'bright Apollo.'

How Apollo came to be connected with Delphi is yet another tale which must be told.

For it was said that when Jupiter (Zeus) once wished to ascertain the central point of the earth, he dispatched two eagles (or two crows). They took flight in opposite courses from sunrise to sunset and met at Delphi, which place was thenceforward titled "the navel of the earth" with an "umbilicus" represented in white marble within its temple.

While such marked Delphi as a place of great reknown, it was not until a shepherd named Coretas discovered that whenever his sheep visited a particular spot, they bleated and gambolled more frequently. It was he who actually found the naturally flowing fumes which enabled the oracle to go into trance.

Legend held that when Coretas himself approached the source of the subterranean fumes, he was seized immediately with ecstasy, and uttered words which were judged inspired.

Not coincidentally, it was on this very same spot that the child Apollo had killed a dragoness, which later tradition changed into a male snake, or python.

In time, a young virgin girl was chosen to interpret Apollo's utterings, and a sylvan bower of laurel branches was erected over the spot from which the fumes arose.

Eventually, a marble temple followed and the priesthood of Delphi arose in which the Pythoness sat on a tripod-like throne, breathing in the divine "afflatus" in order to render Apollo's utterances!

In order to prepare herself, the Pythoness first drank out of a nearby sacred fountain (Castalia), which was reserved for her use alone, and in which she bathed her hair. She also chewed a laurel leaf and encircled her brow with a laurel crown.

During the early days, the oracle spoke only during one month of the entire year, "Byssus," and at first only on the seventh day of that month called "Polypthonus," the birthday of Apollo.

Later on, due to popular demand, the oracle remained open year round, except for three months in the winter when it was held that Apollo was away visiting his special people, the Hyperboreans, who danced, sang and feasted in his honor.

According to the historian Diodorus, originally strict virginity was required of any would-be Pythoness, due to the purity of this state, its traditional connection with the goddess Diana, and the belief that virgins were best suited to keep the oracular mysteries secret and inviolate.

However, as it would happen, one of the consecrated damsels and guardians of the temple found herself visited "by the unicorn," causing the priesthood to abandon this custom in favor of the use of middle-aged women, over fifty, who were simply dressed in maiden's garb!

Persons seeking answers had first to write their questions in a special notebook which was then handed to the Pythoness. Of course, the answers which were given in Greek were often obscure and confusing. To the ancient Greeks, however, such was more than satisfactory since they believed that a god like Apollo did not answer man's questions directly.

Furthermore, while the inquirer was allowed to listen to the reading of his question and the medium's answer; it was the duty of the priest to interpret correctly the answer's true meaning.

Should the inquirer be an ambassador presenting a political question, one can only guess at the priest's motive behind his interpretation of each answer.

During the 4th and 5th centuries B.C., the minimum charge for consulting the oracle was the equivalent of two day's wages for an average Athenian. In addition, freewill offerings as well as traveling expenses were required. If one happened to represent a state or government, ten times the rate for private persons was charged!

On those days that consultations were offered, they were conducted from sunrise to sunset, with two or three women acting as mediums on a shift basis, due to the exhausting nature of the work.

If there were more inquirers than time allowed, some would leave with their questions unanswered until another day, or perhaps even next year!

While actual positions in the queue were determined by ballot, "special" state dignitaries or persons were granted an honorary precedence and higher place in line.

It was at Delphi that Apollo and his priests maintained great influence both in Greek politics and morality. Carved on a column in the foretemple of Delphi were the three famous maxims, or "programmes," of the ancients which have come down to us even today ... KNOW THYSELF ... NOTHING IN EXCESS ... GO SURETY, AND RUIN IS AT HAND!

Although throughout the ancient world, Apollo and the Delphic oracle were known by many names, that of Loxias, 'the ambiguous one,' was the title most often cited. This did not stop Socrates, however, from being a firm believer in the oracle's wisdom; no doubt because Apollo had declared him the wisest of all men, an idea he spent his entire lifetime trying to disprove!

By the 5th century B.C., Delphi's power began to decline, primarily due to various attacks on its credulity brought by a number of prominent figures including Euripides, the Greek dramatist.

Despite its falling from grace, however, Apollo's most famous oracle Delphi persisted well into the Christian era.

It was in 362 A.D. that the Emperor Julian, attempting to restore paganism after Christianity had become the official religion of the Byzantines, sent his physician Oribasius for what was destined to be the final pronouncement of the oracle.

"Tell the king that the curiously built temple has fallen to the ground, that bright Apollo no longer has a roof over his head, or prophetic laurel, or babbling spring. Yes, even the murmuring water has dried up."

And so with these words the Oracle at Delphi was silenced forever!

But while the Delphi of old is gone, the new Delphi reborn by Patricia Hayes and Marshall Smith continues to flourish and prosper.

Of this their special 'Delphi dream,' Patricia has written:

> *Delphi is indeed a spiritual womb where*
> *one can retreat from the busy distractions*

of the world and attune himself to his own spirit. Delphi, in the beautiful mountains of North Georgia, is in the world but not of the world.

There is an easily detectable psychic energy field that surrounds and flows within Delphi. Many miraculous healings, physical, emotional and spiritual, have occurred since Delphi's beginning.

The vision of Delphi is that each student who enters will be able to return home with that same psychic space surrounding them, so that he may probe deeper into the spirit while enclosed in a protective healing energy.

The facilities at Delphi are modern and comfortable in the midst of nature.

Recently, I had an opportunity to sit down with Patricia and Marshall to gather even more information about Delphi and how they plan to develop the 120 acres that currently houses the Delphi Retreat Center in McCaysville, Georgia.

Just as people sought the answers to their questions at ancient Delphi, so people come to Delphi today searching for answers. But time has not stood still.

Today people have far greater awareness and a greater capacity to tap their own inner resources and abilities. Today's Delphi is a place where people come for healing, and in that process answer their own questions, while discovering the splendor and magnificence of their own selves. They are then able to return to their home and maintain a "Delphi Space" of peace and motivation to continue their progress in discovering the wonderful multi-faceted dimensions of their Beings.

The secret of healing lies in the words, "Know Thyself."

You might say one steps into futuristic, more evolved thinking at Delphi than one finds in the everyday world. The reality of our Spiritual Being, a kinship with all life, and the knowledge of Self permeates the environment, the many teachers and activities at Delphi.

Of this Patricia speaks very definitely.....

"Delphi encompasses many forms of healing.

"ETAPH is our educational branch that helps people know and discover themselves. ETAPH stands for Education, Theater, Art, Prosperity, and Healing.

"We will have an Amphitheater, just like the one in ancient Greece ... built into the side of a mountain. Here we will have workshops taught by aware, well-known movie personalities. The workshop participants will produce plays based on traditional myths and archetypes within our consciousness. The plays will have messages and inspire the many people who travel to this outdoor theater in the woods.

"Participants in the theater workshop will learn creativity, magnetic expression, and the gift of freeing themselves for a greater purpose ... a message for all who come. For many people who have not had the time or energy to delve deeply into themselves through therapy or workshops, Delphi amphitheater will provide an education and inspiration through entertainment.

"On a deeper level, ETAPH provides a variety of transformational workshops. Healing oneself sometimes simply means getting in touch with one's purpose. The development of creativity through right-brained Art, discovering the abundance within Self and experiencing prosperity, becoming healthy, happy and purposeful brings one to a healing state of health. As health, self-esteem and understanding are restored, people want to share their love and wisdom and help others as they were helped.

"Delphi has a Healing Passage where people can spend time, allowing nature to return them to the simplicity of life and the beauty of their own hearts. Individuals can make the passage themselves or in a group with a guide.

"There are shifts in energy all along the path of the Passage. At each shift, people experience a feeling of going deeper into themselves. They move beyond the trivia and noisy chatter of conscious thoughts into greater depths within their mind. They become sensitive and able to feel their hearts. At this point the preparation for healing begins.

"The Passage encompasses physical sites, each based on a metaphor, such as the Transition Bridge. This is an actual bridge individuals must cross. As they cross, they actually transform their energies by recalling all of the positive strengths and assets they have in this life or others.

"They intentionally leave behind their tensions, anxieties, fears and doubts, and draw into their energy fields the abilities and positive qualities they desire to have in their new spaces.

"This new space is reached when they have crossed the bridge and step onto land. The energy they have gathered immediately begins to attract loving, positive people and situations into their lives. This Law of Attraction has been known to Initiates for eons.

"The Healing Passage is a metaphor to help individuals learn to create their own metaphors, their own meanings. When they return home, they can begin to create their own healing passages; so they will now have places in the physical world where they can relate with the healing spirit on a daily basis.

"The spirit side of our nature is most practical. Developing the Higher Self means more abundance on every level. It means expressing kindness, consideration, forgiveness, beauty, knowing, wisdom, love and understanding to all persons and forms of consciousness.

"With this expression, we feel abundance, value and self-esteem. We are free to love who we truly are. We are free 'To Be' for the first time in our lives.

"There is a special path on the Healing Passage where one can visit and spend time with many aspects of his or her own consciousness. Pythagoras taught his students about the heroes and gods of history so they could sense and begin to imagine the potential of human consciousness. This helped them eliminate the doubts, fears and anxieties that prevented them from attaining their full potential as human beings.

"There are Healing Springs on the passage. People have experienced many miraculous physical, emotional and mental healings here. The lumps on a woman's breasts disappeared while at this site. This is the site symbolized by the Heart Chakra, where one comes to the realization that he can be healed, and that his life DOES have meaning and purpose.

"There must be preparation for any healing. The Healing Passage provides that time necessary for healing to take place. The insight, understanding, sensitivity and awareness that is reached as one travels the Healing Passage all lead to this actual healing and subsequent changes in physical, emotional and mental states.

"Also at Delphi is found The ROHUN INSTITUTE.

"This branch of Delphi assists those who have reached a point of awareness where they value self-knowledge and transformation. They are ready to change those negative thoughts that are imprisoning them and causing havoc in their lives. These visitors to Delphi want to spiritually evolve and attain their highest selves.

"Many come to Delphi to receive RoHun. Others come to learn how to help others through becoming RoHun therapists, while they help themselves.

"The RoHun Institute has therapists all over the world who help people evolve and awaken to the gifts within their own Spirit, gifts which lie within each of us. The ability to Know Self, the ability to heal, to love, to experience a kinship with all forms of life and, most importantly, to value, respect and love Self are all realized in RoHun. One experiences a sense of the Divine within, and begins to awaken to a sense of Purpose.

"The PATRICIA HAYES SCHOOL OF INNER SENSE DEVELOPMENT and THE ARTHUR FORD INTERNA-TIONAL ACADEMY OF MEDIUMSHIP are the branches of Delphi that train those who wish to develop and use their spiritual abilities to help other people through channeling.

"In these Schools we teach individuals to attune to the many higher dimensions of consciousness in order to channel insightful information and understanding to those who are searching. Students learn to channel energy through color and motion, and provide information through Psychic Art.

"Students become sensitive to non-physical energy and learn to interpret it. This allows them to conduct Psychic Investigations assisting police, archeologists and others seeking information; and most important, to help people relieve grief by knowing that their loved ones continue to exist after the death of their physical bodies.

"Healing is the purpose of developing mediumship, or channeling, as it is now often called. Students learn to channel harmony as they attune to the God Source, and work with souls on other levels to channel healing, whatever the need.

"Students move deeper into Self-Knowledge and magnify their own natural abilities giving them confidence, expertise and professionalism to utilize their abilities in helping others.

"Delphi is a physical place. It is also an energy zone on our planet where people can come to experience spiritual energies that are not often experienced in our mentally oriented materialistic society.

"Delphi is a LIGHTHOUSE in a sense. It calls those home who are looking but can't find what they are looking for in material things and people. It calls one home to the Heart and realization of the Divine.

"So many people have the same comment when they first arrive at Delphi... 'It feels like home!' They don't understand 'Why' until they are ready to go home. They know then that Delphi represents the LOVE that was always in their hearts. They just didn't know how to find it.

"Delphi nourishes individuals and accepts them as they are, and thus frees them to express the POWER of their LOVE.

"The door is opened to the heart. They dance HEART TO HEART. The intensity and power of the energy they experience at Delphi allows them to go home and continue to remember that they are Divine Beings. Their strength and protection in this world, where many unaware beings live, is LOVE.

"Students are able to return home and begin helping others, which provides a way of continual growth for them, whether they have come to the school to bring healing to their own homes and lives, or to professionally help others. They return home with expanded vision, knowledge of their psychic ability and the ability to use it in practical ways. Above all they now have an 'open heart' that has experienced a depth of love not previously felt.

"There are many steps of awareness or progress in one's Journey to Wholeness, and these steps throughout spiritual history have been recognized through Initiation. Initiation is an important part of one's progress. We have a special Initiation Room, as well as a Healing Sanctuary, at Delphi to which people come from everywhere once a month for a Healing Service. Here Spirit Doctors work through channels to bring about healing.

"The EXTENSION OF LIFE FOUNDATION is also located at Delphi. This Branch educates people in the idea of 'Life after death' and the continuation of consciousness. It researches and assists people who have had 'near death' experiences to understand the changes that have occurred.

"Arthur Ford, world renowned medium, channeled the book 'EXTENSION OF LIFE,' through Marshall and myself a few years ago. Arthur's physical body died in 1971. His research on the other side and his knowledge of what happens the moment the physical body dies has helped thousands of individuals.

"The ENOCH FOUNDATION founded by Mauricio Panisset, the Brazilian healer who has light come from every part of his body while he heals, is also at Delphi. People come from everywhere to experience the phenomena of light and healing. Shirley MacLaine wrote about him in her book, 'GOING WITHIN,' and describes the incredible power that emanates from this God-centered man.

"Delphi nourishes the body, mind and spirit. Food for healing, purification, beautification and enjoyment are a part of every pilgrimage to Delphi.

"Delphi will continue to expand. There are over fifty acres soon to be developed including an Enchanted Forest where young children and youth, the leaders of our future, will be able to learn about their Inner Selves as well as the physical world. They will discover the abilities they have to lead us into a peaceful, harmonious joy-fulfilled future. Production of movies for children and the establishment of an academic school will begin soon.

"People come to Delphi and participate in the various programs from all over the world.

"For those who wish to live and work in the energy of Delphi, we have a residential community.

"Delphi is located on former Cherokee Indian grounds. You can sense the respect for nature and Spirit everywhere. Our 'Red Brothers' of past generations loved the land and acknowledged Spirit. Delphi of today continues their legacy.

"The simple beauty of nature, the singing waters, the sacred grounds profoundly touches people and helps them to remember Joy, Love and Peace. They experience a vision of new health and joyful living that transforms their lives.

"Delphi is in the heart of each of us. It calls us to visit our hearts and to know ourselves in a new and wonderful way. Delphi has become a home away from home for many people who come here. It is a spiritual dimension on our physical earth just as it was in Ancient Greece.

"In conclusion, the essence of our work at Delphi is the bringing together of the Four Major Thought Patterns which are the source of Mankind's evolution ... from the East, Survival of Consciousness and Self Awareness ... from the West, Love and Forgiveness.

"When these four patterns come together within each of us, we experience the God within.

"At Delphi, we provide the environment for this experience to happen!"

When Patricia, Marshall, Daniel Romani, Loryn and myself finished walking along the Healing Passage, Patricia turned to me and added the following which crystallized all the plans for Delphi she had spent the afternoon sharing.

"Delphi has been developed in the only way we know how.

"The only way Marshall and I know how to do something is for it to come from within us!"

I left wondering if Apollo might not have said the very same thing.

CHAPTER FIFTEEN

POST SCRIPT

With an explanation of the "Delphi Dream," I guess we have truly come to the end of our journey, at least for the time being.

Books, like anything else in life, begin with a single IDEA and end with a MEMORY!

While this is true for what you are now reading, it is not so for RoHun itself!

Who can truly say what effect the stories we have told, the struggles we have shared, will have on someone now unknown, who will stumble upon this book and read its contents.

One thing is certain, and that is that RoHun is much more than a Patricia Hayes, a Marshall Smith and a place called Delphi!

Great ideas live lives of their own ... are born, go through adolescence, get married, have children of their own, and die!

Who, in all their wisdom, can say what is "true" or "false" or "where" such ideas come from?

Certainly it is true that if there is a God, it is truly His good pleasure that we use each and every thing in His kingdom. Surely this is what the apostle Timothy meant when he wrote:

> *Study to show thyself approved unto God, a workman that needeth not to be ashamed, rightly dividing the word of truth.*

Il Timothy 2:15

As I look back, it is hard to believe how long and how far I have travelled in my own understanding of what is true and what is not!

Certainly, there is yet a reason, unknown to me, as to why I was chosen at this "time" and "space" to tell the story of RoHun.

As I was leaving Delphi after my first visit, I suddenly brought my car to a halt in front of a squirrel who was sitting eating a nut in the middle of the road.

I stopped the car and sat watching the squirrel.

All of a sudden I knew what this was all about!

Legend holds that the squirrel was the only animal to witness Adam's eating of the apple in the Garden of Eden. At the time it was believed it had the tail of a rat. So shocked was he by seeing this sight that he drew his tail across his eyes to shut it out. As a reward, God gave the squirrel the tail he now possesses.

Perhaps RoHun, like the squirrel's tail, provides the way for us to see and accept spiritually that which we do not wish to recognize as a part of our own nature.

Surely, as day follows night, there can never be light without shadow!

Truly, if Jung has taught us anything it is this!

And so it is.....

"You are at the right place, at the right time, for the right reason."

Persons desirous of obtaining further information concerning RoHun are cordially invited to contact the following address:

The RoHun Institute
The RoHun Professional Association
P.O. Box 70, at Delphi
McCaysville, GA 30555
(404) 492-2772 (As of May 3, 1992, area code is 706)

When you call or write, be sure and tell them that "Zolar sent you!"

OTHER BOOKS BY ZOLAR

Book Of Dreams, Numbers & Lucky Days

Book of The Spirits

Compendium of Occult Theories and Practices

Encyclopedia of Ancient and Forbidden Knowledge

Encyclopedia and Dictionary of Dreams

Encyclopedia of Omens, Signs & Superstitions

Star Mates

It's All In The Stars

Mastermind Consciousness

High Magick

The Delphi White Water River

Delphi Grounds

Delphi Teaching Room

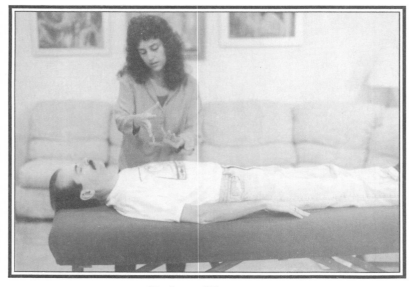

Rohun Therapy